South Africa at War
1939–1945

JACANA POCKET SERIES

The new series of Jacana pocket guides is meant for those who are looking for a brief but lively introduction to a wide range of topics of South African history, politics and biography, written by some of the leading experts in their fields.

Already published

Steve Biko
(by Lindy Wilson)
Shaka
(by Dan Wylie)
Govan Mbeki
(by Colin Bundy)
South Africa's Struggle for Human Rights
(by Saul Dubow)
South Africa at War, 1939–45
(by Bill Nasson)
Ingrid Jonker
(by Louise Viljoen)
Umkhonto weSizwe
(by Janet Cherry)
San Rock Art
(by J.D. Lewis-Williams)
Plague, Pox and Pandemics
(by Howard Phillips)
The ANC Youth League
(by Clive Glaser)
The Idea of the ANC
(by Anthony Butler)

South Africa at War, 1939–1945

A Jacana Pocket History

Bill Nasson

JACANA

In memory of Stephen Watson, and that music in the ice

First published by Jacana Media (Pty) Ltd in 2012

10 Orange Street
Sunnyside
Auckland Park 2092
South Africa
+2711 628 3200
www.jacana.co.za

ISBN 978-1-4314-0382-0

Cover design by Joey Hi-Fi
Set in Minion 10.5/15pt
Printed by Ultra Litho (Pty) Ltd, Johannesburg
Job no. 001864

See a complete list of Jacana titles at www.jacana.co.za

Contents

Preface and acknowledgements 7

1 Some general perspectives 9
2 Caught with its pants down 28
3 Measuring up rather unevenly 41
4 Neutrality averted and early shadow-boxing . . 54
5 Not fighting on the beaches 80
6 What, who, where and why 102
7 Gain, pain and wane 140
8 Postscript: By your feet shall you remember them 153

Select secondary sources and some further reading 155

Index 158

Preface and acknowledgements

Any book on a big event needs to know its limits, especially one as short as this. Naturally, it cannot pretend to be in any way a 'definitive' study, as some wartime topics and themes get short shrift or are not considered. It is not that this volume regards things such as the role of religion in soldiers' lives, or wartime sexuality, or postwar veterans' activity, as uninteresting or unimportant. Rather, the dimensions of the war are just too many and too complex for everything to be touched on in so concise an account.

What *South Africa at War 1939–45* does is to try to offer a brief portrayal of the country's role in the greatest wartime struggle of the past century, and of the impact of that conflict on its society. In other words, this is *not* a history of the world of South Africa in the later 1930s and the 1940s; it is an account of the war effort which the country mounted, and an interpretation of the significance of the Union *at war*. Then, as Jan Smuts reminded British listeners to the BBC's new high-brow radio channel, the Third Programme, in 1946, South Africa had weighed in to help ensure that the future of world affairs would not become, as he had warned in September 1939, black and sinister.

Russell Martin of Jacana first suggested that I write this for the Jacana Pocket series and has been his customary fount of encouragement, helpfulness and editorial good sense ever since. Thanks, too, to Albert Grundlingh for taking time off from his own busy schedule to read the manuscript and suggest some invaluable improvements. The National Museum of Military History in Johannesburg and the National Library in Cape Town generously provided illustrations. I have also to acknowledge the financial assistance of the National Research Foundation towards this research. Opinions and conclusions are, naturally, those of the author and are not necessarily to be attributed to the NRF. Finally, any overview of this kind owes a large debt to numerous scholars upon whose writings I have relied. The bibliography acknowledges a selection of the most useful works.

1

Some general perspectives

Two years after the end of the Second World War, Field-Marshal Jan Smuts, the Union of South Africa's wartime Prime Minister as well as its Minister of External Affairs and Commander-in-Chief of its armed forces, delivered a speech in Johannesburg. Just a few years earlier, Smuts's plate had been extraordinarily full, as his official biographer, the distinguished Australian historian Sir Keith Hancock, later reminded us. For on it lay a 'concentration of political and military power in the hands of one man', without comparison 'anywhere else in the Commonwealth'. Indeed, so interfering and bossy was the Union's leader that he even insisted on personally approving the design of every wartime postage stamp, ensuring that the portrait of an African soldier of the South African Native Military Corps was deleted from a 1941 patriotic portrait set issued to honour South African servicemen and servicewomen. In a way, it told too authentic a story of the local war effort.

Although unusually brief in his August 1947 address for an ambitious man who appreciated few things so much as the sense of his own importance, Smuts, as ever, made a meal of things. Rising to – if not beyond – the occasion, his script for the opening of the country's National War Museum (now the National Museum of Military History) was a reassuring national epic of war readiness and accomplishment. Adolf Hitler, he informed his audience, had 'laughed when he heard that this young nation, so small in population and possessing few great industries', had had the nerve to declare war 'on mighty Germany'.

Yet, thanks to the Union's 'greatest ever united effort', its full-blooded involvement in the Allied war against the Axis powers had charted 'a great chapter in the history of our country'. Fewer 'than three million Europeans' and 'eight million other underdeveloped races' had lined up at a time of crisis and had prevailed together. If anything, the testing experience of war had confirmed South Africa's sacred governing principles. Due to the 'Voortrekker' and 'Pioneer' spirit of its founding 'European elect', the Union's contribution to the most total war of the twentieth century had been disproportionately large. In fact, so much so that it had helped to determine the eventual outcome of hostilities in 1945.

Writing two decades later in the second volume

of his Smuts biography, *The Fields of Force*, Keith Hancock took a slightly more sceptical view. With the comparative dominion experience of his own country as well as those of New Zealand and Canada in mind, he concluded of South Africa's war effort that, when 'viewed from outside', it was 'not massive'. In truth, its participation had been a close run thing and a relief for the Allies that the vital resources of so deeply divided a country had been brought into the war on the right side.

After all, the war had been a troublesome and ambiguous episode, creating no glorious national myths and forging few common bonds. What had it meant? Or, what had it all amounted to? Ultimately, it seemed, to little more than the messy, controversial and unresolved story of a reluctant war. As Hancock concluded in 1966, South Africa's problem at the end of the 1930s was not merely that it was ill-prepared militarily. It was also that it was never fully able to grasp the war which then came. That sense of the Second World War having been more a saga of national half-heartedness than a massive popular effort may be a little sweeping. But it is not without some historical foundation. The point, in short, is that as a belligerent state South Africa was economically steady but politically rocky.

Certainly, its promise was of abundant assets. Territorially, with its League of Nations mandate territory of South West Africa, the Union was a dominion diamond of any British Empire war effort. In addition to those diamonds and the world's largest gold reserves, it possessed crucial deposits of coal, iron ore, manganese, copper and other strategic minerals and raw materials. Moreover, the country was so remote from probable regions of armed conflict that it was likely to get through any major European war with its resources undamaged.

Nor was this all. Like Australia, it had a developing industrial modernity. South Africa's expanding industrial infrastructure contained pockets of advanced technological skills and scientific knowledge. Stimulated particularly by mining, sectors such as chemicals, explosives, metallurgy and optics were highly sophisticated. The engineering foundries and workshops of metal industries, large cold-storage depots, well-constructed rail system, and deep-water harbours and shipping maintenance facilities were other elements ripe for adaptation to war supply and servicing. Clear skies, easy weather and wide fields of vision were ideal for aviation activity, making South Africa a plum spot for pilot and navigation training.

Also capable of rapid expansion was the country's humming manufacturing industry, with metal assembly, textiles, leather goods, canning, bottling and other production ready to spurt. When it came to supplying the war, the Union's energetic role should feature in any story of that gargantuan industrial effort. With massive growth in mining, steel and textiles, industrial output virtually doubled between 1939 and 1945. Factories churned out twelve million pairs of boots, two million steel helmets, almost five million grenades, some 5,800 armoured cars and a fat mass of other war materiel, much of it starting from scratch, including tyres, trucks, barges, portable steel bridges, howitzers, mortars, mines, gunsights, eyeshields and even handcuffs.

Agricultural capacity also endowed South Africa with a strategic importance quite out of scale with its actual fighting efforts. To have been flush in stocks of grain, fruit, livestock and fish counted significantly in a ravenous conflict in which a great deal turned on securing protein and fat. Compared with Germany, Italy and Japan, its enemies with hunger pangs, not only was the Union well lined with food and able to expand its food-processing facilities, particularly in canning and dehydrated products. It also enjoyed a healthy export surplus for the provisioning of the Allied side with everything from apricot jam to bacon, and not least with those items so essential to the morale of British, Australian, New Zealand, Canadian, American and other troops, like confectionery, beer and cigarettes, of which almost two and a half million were dispatched overseas.

Granted, South Africans faced some shortages. Among these were golf balls and white flour, and a hiccup with rice when the Japanese gobbled up British colonial territories in the Far East in the early 1940s. But, in any event, all that lingering rice shortages did was to produce a curry crisis for Indian and Muslim communities. Getting through the war without severe belt-tightening was one of the most striking features of South Africa's war effort.

It mattered, not least of all, because that food dividend became a strategic asset in a titanic conflict in which, as the historian Lizzie Collingham has argued recently in her book *The Taste of War: World War Two and the Battle for Food* (2011), the balance of endurance and survival and the sustaining of morale rested in large measure on the adequate filling of stomachs. Indeed, immediately after 1945, when vitamins were deficient, South Africa could still provide a remedy. One quaint answer to short rations in austerity Britain was the importation of millions of tins of South African *snoek* in 1947–8. Unfortunately, as British stomachs were revolted by *snoek piquante* (as it was popularly dubbed), a despairing Ministry of Food ended up advising consumers to inflict the fish on their cats. For a nation famous for its animal lovers, that must have been a moral challenge.

When, on the other hand, we turn from healthy

producing *for* the war to local feelings *about* the war, we encounter a very different picture. Acutely divided, South African society was framed by brittleness and schism rather than cohesive strength and unanimity. For one thing, the bulk of the majority black population of African, Coloured and Indian inhabitants were hardly animated by war concerns, and certainly displayed little inclination to fall into a voluntary war effort or to wave flags, sing songs or otherwise adopt the war in their imagination. As with the Union's expeditionary involvement in an earlier world war, here was another European conflict of that remote sort, as unlikely as the last to show anything by way of recognition and reward for black patriotic service and sacrifice. Some did join up again, mostly from the ranks of the impoverished. But they were not exactly in the lead.

For another thing, a large portion of the dominant white minority was vigorously anti-war. Not necessarily pacifist in any ideological sense or organised form, this infectious sentiment displayed more than one symptom. For some, being anti-war certainly meant a preference for peace and for neutrality. For others, though, it meant being anti-*British* and thus, to one or other degree, either implicitly or explicitly pro-*German*. Embittered by the anglicising outcome of the 1899–1902 Anglo-Boer struggle, many Afrikaners would neither identify with, nor join, what they viewed as another British imperialist war and the cause of an alien British Crown. Ultimately, only English-speaking whites and a loyalist tributary of Anglo-Afrikaners, or 'King's Afrikaners', were prepared, enthusiastically and unequivocally, to take up arms and donate their bodies to the needs of London. For other ordinary Afrikaners, war service was work, not commitment but a snatched relief from joblessness and poverty.

Equally, none of this is to suggest that life in the Union was so insular as to have been left untouched by the issues of the 'crisis of civilisation' which so consumed the well-to-do intelligentsia and the political elite of European societies in the prewar 1930s. Fringe political constituencies on both left and right were internationally minded. On the Marxist left, the Communist Party of South Africa rallied around anti-Fascist causes, like that of the Republic in the Spanish Civil War of 1936–9, while the Trotskyist and mainly Coloured National Liberation League (NLL) translated European Fascism to the domestic political context, explaining white minority rule as a brand of villainous *herrenvolkism*, or master-race oppression. Those to their European right included pro-Mussolini immigrant Italians who held Blackshirt picnics in Cape Town and Johannesburg to celebrate the birthdays of Il Duce. Elsewhere, the growing difficulties of the international system were reflected in the English and Afrikaans press and entered parliamentary politics, the preoccupations of extra-parliamentary bodies, societies, lecture halls and other arenas of public discussion.

Crises in Europe and elsewhere in Africa also drew some local people into direct action. Thus, in protest at Italy's colonial invasion of Abyssinia in 1935–6, unionised workers at Cape Town docks refused to handle Italian ships. Similarly, the outbreak of civil war in Spain saw the anti-Franco cause supported by funds and supplies raised by the Communist Party and trade unions. Some South Africans of internationalist inclination also volunteered to fight in Spain, notably the leading Afrikaans and English writers Uys Krige and Roy Campbell, the former throwing in his lot with the republican Popular Front and the latter joining Franco's Catholic nationalist cause. Some of the most searing, moving and internationally influential coverage of the criminality of the second Italo-Abyssinian War and the Spanish Civil War came from the eminent, London-based South African war correspondent George Steer.

Still, distant overseas conflagrations depicted by Steer in *The Times* could scarcely be said to have gripped a national public mood, any more than did even the ominous Czech crisis of early 1939. Indeed, there is very little to suggest that South African society was edging towards any general acceptance that war was imminent and that involvement in it as a British dominion was a distinct possibility. Inevitably, then, without a meaningful psychological alignment, there was no popular mandate for war in September 1939.

Even so, the war did bite, and South Africa went on to become a not insignificant Allied belligerent, negotiating its engagement in hostilities in ways that were mostly glancing but sometimes deep. And the measure of its positive contribution was certainly also of sufficient significance for leading British Second World War historians such as Richard Overy to recognise the Union's role in propping up London's war effort. As he has again emphasised in the 2010 edition of *The Battle of Britain*, the myth of British society fighting alone by 1940 rests on a complete disregard of 'the vital and substantial support of Canada, South Africa, Australia, New Zealand, India and the colonial empire'. In numbering South Africans among those whose 'participation had been paramount' to the British Empire war effort, Norman Davies takes the same tack in his *Europe at War 1939–45* (2006).

This takes us back to our two opening points or, simply, the obvious gap between political rhetoric and historical reality. In his 1947 estimation, Jan Smuts was undoubtedly over-egging a comparatively modest dish.

For that matter, a more sober Keith Hancock may well have been diminishing unduly the size of that portion. Where, then, does the balance lie?

Perhaps, as in so many things, it is somewhere in between. There too, perhaps, lies something of the distinctiveness of South Africa's war experience. It was neither invaded nor occupied. Its economy not only fared well, it prospered from the war. There was no transformative political upheaval or social revolution. Not merely did it escape the horrific violence and destruction and the plunging unpredictabilities of the Second World War. There was virtually no war-related bloodshed on its own soil.

The reality of being in a world at war was thus mostly a second-hand experience, a simmering 'phoney war'. It is worth underlining the modest scale of mobilisation. In all, just over 334,000 inhabitants volunteered for full-time war service. Of these, roughly 132,000 whites and 123,000 African and Coloured recruits served in land forces. About 9,500 whites did duty in the navy, while some 44,600 served in the air force. Branches of the female Auxiliary Defence Corps enlisted just over 21,000 white women, while some 3,700 others worked in the Military Nursing Service. In this respect, only a tiny fraction of South Africa's people *fought* the war or assisted in prosecuting its national war effort. Moreover, at the sharp end, an even smaller fraction was released for service beyond the Union's northern borders. The ratio of losses, too, was low, with a casualty count of nearly 9,000 killed, over 8,000 wounded and more than 14,000 taken prisoner. It was the human chart of death, suffering and pain. But it was not unbearable carnage.

Yet, at the same time, things were shaken up. There were panics over the threat of invasion, anxieties over preparedness for war production, fears over domestic order and social peace, and worries over how to manage a war effort that failed to command a national consensus. All deeply felt, they provide an essential part of the context within which to bring the 1939–45 war into view. This matters, not least because the general history of South Africa's Second World War has long been something of a shrinking story.

Rather, it is nineteenth-century colonial land or frontier wars, rebellions or wars of empire that provide the usual subject-matter of local historical dramas. South Africa's professional historians have tended also to have other, bigger fish to fry, such as interpretations of segregation and apartheid. Growing international condemnation of apartheid in later postwar decades also marginalised the history and memory of South Africa's stand and performance in the Second World War. An increasingly distasteful and embarrassing presence, the country no longer fitted into an Allied and Commonwealth war of pride and honour, its profile fading further at each solemn gathering to pay tribute to 1940s sacrifice and achievement.

In international historical writing, too, recognition of the Union's participation has been waning in recent global histories of 1939–45. Gerhard Weinberg's *A World at Arms: A Global History of World War II* (1994) at least finds space for Smuts, who was, after all, one of Britain's field-marshals and a member of Winston Churchill's Imperial War Cabinet. M.R.D. Foot and I.C.B. Dear's *The Oxford Companion to the Second World War* (1995) has more of value, if of an encyclopaedic kind, in Ian Phimister's thumbnail sketch. Closer to the present, though, South Africa's involvement has come to look increasingly like a case of the disappearing dominion or, perhaps, of the dominions coming up one short. Gordon Martel's edited *The World War Two Reader* (2004) omits South Africa, as does Evan Mawdsley's *World War II: A New History* (2009). No longer are the war years reduced to Smuts. It is almost as though the Union's experience has been expunged from the overall historical record of 1939–45.

Leaving aside what international histories may be saying – or, more, *not* saying – there is another, more speculative question to be asked. It is about what – if *any* – images of the war remain in the wider historical consciousness or in the memory of South Africans. Assuming that some encompassing sense of that past exists, it might well be asked, what meaning does the world war now have? Or, perhaps yet more fundamentally, in what way is it remembered at all?

Leaving aside the contentious European and American interpretations, if one were, say, Australian, or Indian, or Canadian or Ethiopian, one intriguing question might be what interpretation of the 1940s is being transmitted to you today. For South Africa, on the other hand, it could be a case not merely of what version – of *whose* war, or of *which* people's war – but of *what* war? Was it then that demobilised African soldiers were paid off with bicycles, or was that in 1918? When was it that letters had to have those miniature stamps?

If the clash of 1939–45 sounds a minor note in South Africa's history, at some other introspective levels it may also not be all that surprising. Indubitably, knowledge and remembrance of past modern wars, including the border wars of the apartheid era, have always, in various ways, become connected to the shifting politics of the present. In that sense, just as the Civil War has long been a contested past in Spain, so South Africa's Second World War has been too mixed a narrative to be pressed into national political service. It has never really presented the temptation of being turned manipulatively by ruling interests into a *usable* war.

Accordingly, after 1948 the new National Party government swiftly won one of its earliest paper wars, that of the archives. It quietly smothered a state project to produce an official history of the Union at war, a venture that had been started in 1940 under the scholar J. Agar-Hamilton, then an army captain in the Union Defence Force (UDF). Commemorating South African involvement in a second British imperial war looked as anachronistic as it was indigestible in the coming-of-age of Afrikaner nationalism after 1945.

Equally, following the dissolution of that apartheid nationalist order in the mid-1990s, the Second World War has been fated still to remain the past of another country. Planted in the moral and emotional landscape of its own liberation struggle, majority-rule black nationalism naturally has scant interest in cultivating memories of an old South Africa's integration into a global European war effort. Above all perhaps, unlike elsewhere, in South Africa the Second World War did not feed into an effective 1950s struggle for decolonisation and national liberation.

Now, to round off with a couple of concluding reflections. The first is that we have been seeing renewed flickerings of interest in the 1940s as a distinctive period of change or transition in South African society. As Saul Dubow and Alan Jeeves argue in their edited volume, *South Africa's 1940s: Worlds of Possibilities* (2005), those seething years and their aftermath generated 'competing visions of the future', as the mingling of 'war overseas and political turmoil at home' rocked 'established certainties' and infused the decade with a 'remarkable sense of fluidity and flux'. While that is indeed so, there still remains the essential scenario of the war *as war*. In that respect, Albert Grundlingh's much earlier depiction of South Africa at war in B.J. Liebenberg and S.B. Spies's edited work *South Africa in the 20th Century* (1993) remains more on the button.

A final point is that many South Africans of my generation grew up and had part of our childhood consciousness in the 1950s and 1960s formed by diverting household stories and memories of the Second World War. Today, we live – and our children will doubtless continue to live – with some of the consequences of where the outcome of that war might have taken South Africa, and where it eventually went. Then, though, the war that was passed on was an almost carnival episode of blackouts, boozy Australian soldiers ransacking shops, and German submarines doing their dirty business out in the bay before bolting.

Early postwar decades were also tinted with an odd array of stock images handed down by adults as anecdotes, sometimes poignant, but more often sardonic or funny. In my own life, these included

General Hertzog, stranded Vichy French sailors, Field-Marshal Smuts, Just Nuisance, Dr Malan, Montecassino, Tobruk, General Dan Pienaar, the Lady in White, the Ossewabrandwag, Abyssinia, U-boats, Egypt, Italian tanks (one forward gear, six reverse), visiting Royal Air Force pilots, Robey Leibbrandt, bushcarts, Sailor Malan, the Cape Corps, rice queues, Stormjaers, Koffiefontein, Radio Zeesen, Oswald Pirow, BBC war broadcasts, Ouma Smuts, treason, Italian prisoners of war, Montgomery of Alamein, Vera Lynn on the English Service, the 'Carry On' English film comedian Sid James (ex-South African Army lieutenant), and the *Hobbit* fantasy author, J.R.R. Tolkien, who came from the Orange Free State and had gone on to be a British spy (in fact, a 1939 code-breaker). There was also life under Smuts or life as it was, then, *before* apartheid. Of much that was mocking, there was little to beat the Axis humiliation of General Klopper, possibly more desert 'dassie' than Desert Rat.

To pause there is also to be reminded that it was never more so than in the wartime 1940s that modern South Africa was perceived internationally to be just another country, neither especially flawed nor particularly controversial. Along with Australia, New Zealand, Canada and India, it was counted among the angels. Indeed, it was even more welcome for having risen above itself. For, whatever its domestic political controversies over involvement in the war, whatever its handicapping Afrikaner nationalist faults, it was still more virtuous than one other dominion state, a disloyally neutral Ireland.

Such was the basis on which Humphrey Bogart, Bing Crosby and Gracie Fields remembered the Smuts household in December 1944. From a California studio they broadcast seventy-fourth birthday greetings to Mrs Isie Smuts, commending the doings of her Gifts and Comforts Fund for South Africa's troops. Praising Pretoria's answer to Eleanor Roosevelt, Fields even sang *Vat Jou Goed en Trek, Ferreira* in passable Afrikaans, addressing it to Ouma. It is a pity that a silver-tongued Crosby missed out on a rendition of his 1940s *White Christmas.* That might have been no less folksy, if also spot on in another way.

Celebrated by Hollywood celebrities, wartime South Africa was still seeing out its earlier life as another country. It even continued to enjoy a further cinematic after-life in that classic 1958 British drama about Tobruk and the desert war, *Ice-Cold in Alex.* One of its leading characters, played by Anthony Quayle with an Afrikaans accent rather less credible than that of Gracie Fields, was the gruff and wily Captain Van der Poel.

Yet, even today, there are times when, suddenly and unexpectedly, that past stops being another country.

Writing in the London *Independent* in April 2011, the noted journalist Robert Fisk assessed the fluctuating fortunes of the Libyan rebel campaign against Colonel Muammar Gaddafi's regime. It was, he concluded, 'far more retreating' than even 'General Klopper did in the Libyan desert in the 1940s'. Teasingly, Fisk nudged his more baffled readers, 'Yes, James, go on, look him up.' We, too, can now go on to look him up and see something of what else besides made up South Africa's experience of, and contribution to, the Second World War.

2

Caught with its pants down

With armed service in its ranks ordinarily restricted to men identified as being 'of European descent', the creation of the UDF under the South Africa Defence Act in 1912 followed the formation two years earlier of the Union of South Africa. It marked the culmination of Britain's gradual military withdrawal from its newest dominion, after the end of the South African War in 1902. Some minor British army parties lingered, Royal Navy (RN) personnel saw to the strategic Cape port facility of Simonstown, and there was continuing routine liaison between Pretoria and London over defence and security matters. Yet, these aside, the departure of Britain's military presence was virtually complete but for the institutional symbolism that it left behind. In its military ethos and culture of command, the Anglo-Afrikaner UDF was glued in place by English. But khaki had become South African.

In 1914, whatever the strength of local neutrality

and anti-war sentiment, Britain's declaration of war against Germany made the Union a belligerent, committing it constitutionally to hostilities. Thereafter, however, the Crown could not count for very much longer on such obligatory compliance in time of war. Of great importance for future war-making powers was the passing by the British parliament of the 1931 Statute of Westminster, which sealed the effective legislative independence of the dominions. Three years later, the South African parliament passed the Status of Union Act, confirming a position of legal sovereignty in which no act of the British parliament could be binding on the Union unless it was agreed to by its own legislature. By then, of course, security needs and strategic policy had been South Africa's business for virtually two decades.

Accordingly, in the 1920s and 1930s, defence matters and other military concerns, such as the acquisition of equipment and supplies, merely became part of routine political transactions between South African and British governments, or else dotted the agendas of humdrum conference exchanges and committee meetings involving London and its self-governing 'white' Commonwealth states. Still, not everyone was sanguine about defence preparedness being left in so loose a state. In 1935, the year in which the Prime Minister, General J.B.M. Hertzog, announced that he was not prepared to be part of any general scheme of imperial defence, a retired British naval service intelligence officer did some local snooping. In an anonymous account carried by the London *Evening Standard* in November of that year, he described South African claims of maintaining adequate coastal defences as 'so empty as to be laughable'. Air force strength was 'deplorable', sea defence was 'barely detectable' and the army was little more than 'larger than the usual sort of Boer commando, if at least decently spruced up'. All in all, the UDF was about as imposing as a 'provincial French gendarmerie'.

While this litany of deficiencies may have been greatly exaggerated, he had a point. This had been grasped as far back as 1921 by Smuts in a parliamentary argument for a well-armed peace, without which 'any enemy' could 'come to our shores and pluck South Africa like a ripe fruit'. The Union was a significant peg on London's lines of trade and communications with the further reaches of empire. If insecure in a crisis, it could be vulnerable against any country with maritime capacity and a taste for action – for defence planners in the interwar era, these included not only Italy and France but even, for a time, the United States of America.

How would South Africa face up to such potential perils? Clearly, it lacked the men, the equipment, the ships and the aircraft to hold its lengthy coastline, to protect its ports and territorial waters, and to defend its extensive and exposed land borders. Nor was it displaying much intention of shoring up its rickety defence establishment – on the contrary. Oswald Pirow, the influential Minister of Defence from 1933, warned more than once that the electorate would not stomach any wasteful increases in defence spending, estimating in 1934 that by 1938–9 a politically tolerable annual limit of £1 million would have been reached. It was not only the Great Depression which was curbing arms spending but also electoral worries over the consequences of military matters seen to be getting out of hand.

The government shrugged off press accusations in the *Cape Times* and *The Star* that its behaviour was resembling that of the proverbial ostrich with its head in the sand, as well as revelations that its defence estimate represented only around a paltry £1 in every £35 of national expenditure. While far from spoiling for war, the country was ready for any armed challenges. Still, the Minister of Defence did not take kindly to being caught on the hop. Prompted by mounting anxieties over the adequacy of war preparedness, in July 1938 a cheeky Cape MP, Sydney Waterson, reminded the House of Assembly that the Minister of Defence had failed to provide parliament with any information

Rather soft on the Third Reich: Oswald Pirow and his wife, Else Piel. (National Library of SA, Cape Town)

on defence since two perfunctory announcements in 1934 and 1936. Waterson then asked – rhetorically – if the country possessed a single modern anti-aircraft battery. Stung, a disconcerted Pirow evaded answering but ensured that Waterson got paid for his trouble. Several months later, he was plucked from parliamentary combat and posted to France on less bothersome diplomatic duties.

It was Oswald Pirow who, more than anyone else, embodied personally the difficulties and the predicament of military preparation and planning. By the mid-1930s, he had a trundling plan for army and air force expansion behind which lay some woefully misconceived military assumptions, including the dismissal of any serious threat from the sea. In June 1935, his fanciful thinking was revealed to the UDF General Staff. By and large, an invasion was improbable, although there was *some* chance of a seaborne landing or a land attack from the north with air support. Far more worrying, though, was the spectre of major African restiveness or rebellion. Sketching a plot which echoed the most classic of John Buchan's contemporary thrillers about civilisation and decay, the Minister of Defence foresaw Africans in Central Africa being seduced by an unholy alliance between Bolshevism and Islam, a subversive tide that could lap down into the Union. Some other calculations were even more woolly. It was conceivable that Britain could go to war with France or, possibly, with Japan. Italy was discounted as a threat in Africa, with France identified as the chief menace. Yet the greatest risk of all in Africa would be a Franco-Italian offensive alliance.

For Pirow, a forceful exponent of the expansion of South African influence into British white settler Africa, armed mobilisation was another test for his 'South Africa First' ideology. Sceptical of the value to the UDF of European fighting organisation and conventions, by 1938 he was still clinging to the conviction that the ability to stop any enemy would depend ultimately on land forces operating in the bush or plugging the coastline. In keeping with commando tradition and the tactical inheritance of mobility and initiative, the army would be trained in light, raiding columns in preparation for widespread bush warfare.

Transport would not require any costly modernisation of the country's arthritic fleet of British military lorries, which dated from the end of the First World War. Instead, it would be provided by an indigenous contraption of which the Minister of Defence was inordinately proud – an ox-drawn 'bush barrow', derided almost immediately as a bushcart by incredulous military veterans. While war was by then known to be hell, there was no desire to go there in a bushcart. Still, despite scornful critics having a field day, Pirow dug in his heels and refused to fund anything else. By March 1938, there had been some lumbering experiments in army mobility, but the idiosyncratic cart programme was doomed from its inception and few finished vehicles were produced. This came as a relief to the apprehensive generals of the Union's Defence Council, to say nothing of the *afrikaner* oxen of the Transvaal.

All political careers have their embarrassing moments. In the run-up to war, Oswald Pirow had quite a few from which to choose. They included the Deputy

Prime Minister, Jan Smuts, confidentially urging the visiting British Cabinet Secretary, Sir Maurice Hankey, to be wary of him as he was suspected of being too cosy with Pretoria's German diplomats. But the top slot is not hard to fill. Rearmament with bushcarts went beyond amateur misjudgement and turned Pirow into a laughing-stock, a figure for cartoon and caricature in the English press of the late 1930s.

The pantomime of bush war preparation was made even worse by an arms-buying visit to Britain in October 1938. 'Rummage' was all that could be bought, Pirow grumbled, informing Paris embassy staff that what London was offering was bows and arrows with which to shoot lions. Brigadier Pieter de Waal, Director of Military Training and no fan of his political master, was reminded that Pirow had *himself* once advocated that fleet South African infantry could be equipped with bows and arrows. It was another bizarre story. Still, perhaps the 1944 battle of Montecassino might then have gone on to become South Africa's Agincourt, and Oswald Pirow its Henry V.

While the Defence Minister dithered over entirely ineffectual military Five Year Plans, the second of which was due for completion in 1941, the alarming tone of newsreels and radio reports on worsening conditions in Europe spurred on voluntary civilian mobilisation. Women were prominent from the start, with the South African Red Cross Society organising a Women's National Service Legion which, by the end of 1938, had enlisted over 7,000 white volunteers for nursing, welfare, administrative and other auxiliary war work.

The Minister of Defence welcomed these and other amateur efforts, such as those by motor traders and wireless technicians to register for communications duties. Unsurprisingly, he purred over the registration of Johannesburg sportsmen. Pirow had been a javelin-throwing champion and was no mean hand at other manly pursuits such as hunting, fencing, wrestling and boxing – the last being the one and only thing he had in common at the time with Nelson Mandela.

But in the more crucial respect of ensuring that his country was organised and equipped to fight a modern war, to all essential purposes Pirow left it on the ropes. His was scarcely the state of mind necessary for what was coming up. It would not turn out to be merely a short-range land and air campaign to hold enemies at bay. It would entail the development of a long expeditionary reach into the theatres of East Africa, the Western Desert and southern Italy, and the maintenance of a high level of domestic vigilance.

Never much of a winning figure, Oswald Pirow is today little remembered in the historical record other than as a crude Afrikaner nationalist and pre-apartheid white supremacist. There is, however, less cause for him to be forgotten as the founder in 1934 of South African Airways (SAA), Africa's first national airline. Equipped with modern and efficient German Junkers aircraft, an able and ambitious Pirow broke South African dependence on Britain's technically inferior Imperial Airways services. So much so, in fact, that by the time war began, SAA was more than matching British commercial air power in the Rhodesias and in East Africa. In that regard, although a studiously pedestrian figure in rearmament, he had more than one string to his bow.

Yet, Pirow's distrusted image as a renegade and as pro-German or actually pro-Nazi was not exactly undeserved. Commentators in the *Rand Daily Mail*, *Natal Witness* and other papers in late 1938 and early 1939 even accused him of intentionally starving the country of proper steel in order to soften it up for an invading enemy. For a government minister it went, for one agitated observer in the *Cape Times* in December 1938, beyond appeasement into virtual 'treason' or 'criminal subversion'. British satirists, too, weighed in during a 1938 European visit on which Pirow rubbed shoulders with Hitler, Mussolini, Franco and the Portuguese dictator, Antonio Salazar. In the *Evening Standard* of November that year, the prominent political cartoonist David Low lampooned him as a burly ballet dancer entertaining Hitler, Goering and Ribbentrop, doing a 'Pirowette' clad in a swirling paper tutu of maps of Africa showing lost German colonies restored.

Echoing her father's Germanophilia, in June 1939 Pirow's daughter caused a fuss during a visit to London by telling the *Daily Express* that the family household was proudly German-speaking and felt *more German* than South African. Three years previously, he had visited Berlin and had delighted the local press with his ferocious anti-communism and assurance that there was little support in South Africa for spending on rearmament against Germany – no serious thought was being given to it as a future enemy.

Pirow also attended the 1936 Berlin Olympic Games where he cheered on the Springbok boxing team. Its champion heavyweight was a policeman and former cadet soldier named Sidney Robey Leibbrandt. Like Pirow, he made no secret of the fact that he was partial to Nazi Germany, staying on after the Games to throw himself into that most airborne of Aryan pursuits, gymnastics, and to qualify later in paragliding in the German army.

Much has been made, in books such as Brian Bunting's *The Rise of the South African Reich* (1969), of Oswald Pirow's adulation of Hitler, whom he described as *ein heiliger* (a saint), and as 'the greatest man of his day, perhaps the greatest of the last thousand years'. For all that, it should be kept in mind that on this score the South African Minister of Defence was scarcely unique. Not only before but into the early years of the war, even Britain had its own mixed crop of Nazi-German appeasers. Among those who endorsed peace with Hitler were pacifists, fascist fellow-travellers, the communists and fascists who found themselves turned into odd bedfellows by the August 1939 Nazi–Soviet Pact, military strategists, politicians and some senior Foreign Office officials. Myopic admiration of the Führer extended to David Lloyd George, the outstanding British First World War leader who, well into 1940, was still counting him 'among the greatest leaders of men in history'.

Having left the Union chronically underarmed, by mid-1939 Pirow was being accused of having abandoned national sovereignty in favour of peace at any price. In fairness, it was perhaps just one price, and that being Germany. In a fitting end, the coming German war which had dogged him through the 1930s did him in when it came. Pirow supported the failed parliamentary cause of neutrality, and in the following year established his own New Order ultra-right nationalist faction, which backed the formation of an authoritarian one-party state on the Nazi model. Elbowed out in the early 1940s by his more constitutionally inclined Afrikaner nationalist contemporaries, his minuscule proto-fascist New Order became a party. It did not prosper.

Soon out of Union politics as well as out of the war, Oswald Pirow ended up languishing in the political wilderness. There, after 1945 he was nourished for a time by another posturing fundamentalist who had backed the wrong war horse. Sir Oswald Mosley, leader of the British Union of Fascists, joined Pirow in planning a stillborn anti-communist crusade, 'Enemies of the Soviet Union', and in developing a fantastic plan to split the African continent into exclusively black and white regions. Meanwhile, Pirow's rooted affection for Germany remained, reflected in the early 1950s by his writings in the German magazine *Nation Europa*. When it came to Berlin, somehow he could never avoid getting a little carried away.

3

Measuring up rather unevenly

On the eve of war in September 1939, the condition of the UDF at the end of the Pirow tenure was abysmal. Not only did the skinny state of its resources mean that a new army, air force and navy would have to be formed virtually from scratch. Its Chief of the General Staff (CGS), the urbane and industrious Major-General Sir Pierre van Ryneveld, a First World War veteran who had flown in the Royal Flying Corps (RFC), was also stuck with other difficulties.

One was the frustration of Anglo-Afrikaner military life in a place so fractured politically that several of his more insolent brigade commanders did not hesitate to share their personal view with officers that they considered it wrong to be declaring war. Another was the constant meddling of the austere and bony General Smuts who, soon after the declaration of war, artfully inveigled himself into becoming the Union's Commander-in-Chief. Practically, this made

Van Ryneveld operational Chief of Staff to an intrusive figure who constantly interfered in *anything* to do with military matters. This included the Prime Minister keeping a watch on his most personally trusted and favoured General Staff circle. A uniformed Smuts and his uniformed personal favourites knew well who they were, and that theirs was a patronage relationship to be well minded.

Thirdly, the transmission belt of command was a mess. There was no direct, uncluttered chain of communication between Defence Headquarters and units, leading to duplicated or even triplicated orders. In addition, hierarchies of line authority were hazy, and there was no commonly recognised system of coded instruction from higher command through which to ensure that officers down the chain would automatically set about mobilisation, marshalling forces, or even devising emergency local security measures. In brief, the Union lacked an understood script for the armed undertaking which awaited it.

Even more fundamental, given the imperative of coherent planning in modern war, was the fact that the Union's Defence Headquarters had no overall war plan for national defence or for taking on a campaigning role in *any* sort of hostilities. Instead of having a basis for calculating the efforts required for chosen movements, and for laying down logistical needs and what to stockpile, it made impending war an exposed gamble. For a new wartime government that was on the verge of taking power, there was a lot to be overcome and a lot to be devised, and all of it to be done at a truly cracking pace. The shift from semi-torpor to the meeting of immediate war demands – an imposing feat to be accomplished – would turn out to be remarkably effective, as the country sprinted to put together a passable war effort.

The measure of that achievement lies in the steep deficiencies that had to be surmounted. In September 1939 the regular army component of the UDF, the Permanent Force, which had numbered only 1,791 men in 1934, could still muster only 5,385 officers and men. Similarly, the army's part-time territorial formations, like the Active Citizen Force (ACF), the Defence Rifle Associations or Afrikaans Burgher Commandos and ancillary units, consisted effectively of just 13,490 men, with some tens of thousands of members of *skietkommandos*, or commando sharpshooters, mostly a nominal paper asset – if not a paper tiger.

For the most part, these peacetime forces were unprepared for warfare, being neither adequately trained nor properly armed and equipped. On top of acute shortages of modern weaponry such as mortars and Bren guns, army training capacity was dire. Even with training depots halving the length of courses to increase the number of instructors at the end of the 1930s, only some 150 had been passed out and dispersed. South Africa was saved the usual prewar conundrum of military capacity which confronted many countries in 1939, that of betting on quality or quantity. Its hand held neither.

Thus, land force armaments were, without exception, mostly obsolete if not positively antiquated, and with depleted ammunition supplies. Coastal gun batteries for harbours and bays were scratchy, with the shore defence of Durban and Port Elizabeth up to a couple of obsolete pieces clamped to railway trucks of armoured trains. These trains, too, had long passed their better days, those having been spent on Transvaal occupation service under Lord Kitchener in the early 1900s. Mobile field forces had no modern artillery and were equipped with merely 65 run-down guns. By comparison, back in 1899 the Boer republican forces had had an arsenal of almost 100 modern European guns.

Modern armour presented another dismal picture. South Africa had not formed any armoured vehicle units before the arrival of hostilities and all that could be cranked up were two obsolete Vickers tanks and two Crossley armoured cars, which had been imported from Britain in the mid-1920s. When the Crossleys saw a little punitive colonial action in South West Africa in the 1930s, the performance had not been auspicious. Part of a police detachment and air squadron mission dispatched to subdue a recalcitrant Ovambo chief, the armoured cars succumbed to overheating and tyre failure.

That immediate prewar expedition had also involved late 1920s Westland Wapiti biplanes of the South African Air Force (SAAF), which probably provide as good a reference as any for the state of air power. Its handful of more experienced pilots were mostly South African RFC veterans like Kenneth van der Spuy, a chief advocate and founder of the SAAF in the immediate aftermath of the First World War. Like their contemporary British counterparts in post-Ottoman Mesopotamia (Iraq), Wapitis were the workhorses of pacification from the air, suppressing acts of insurrection from the early 1920s.

As Major-General Van der Spuy recounted in his absorbing autobiography, *Chasing the Wind* (1966), his air force 'birds that laid iron eggs' had a 'morally' educative effect upon the rebellious South West African Bondelswarts, and then intimidated the Rehoboth Basters. However, when the target changed from African peasants to urban white miners, it became a more squeamish business. Ordered by Smuts to assist in crushing the 1922 Rand Revolt, 'the new Air Force' experienced 'deep regrets' that 'our own countrymen should be fired upon and bombed from the air'. The SAAF had, thus, been 'blooded' a decade before the war. But its punitive operations had been an easy proposition, providing little tactical preparation for air combat and anti-aircraft defences.

Of the 1,736 men serving in the SAAF at the end of the following decade, over 800 were apprentices in what was essentially an air training body rather than a unit primed for widespread operations in support of land as well as sea forces and for long-range deployment in a battle for aerial supremacy. Indeed, it was not until 1937 that the SAAF acquired its own air directorate. This in itself did not imply much by way of capability. There was, for example, no aerial reconnaissance of the sea-lanes around the Union's lengthy coastline of over 2,500 kilometres, with an exposed South West Africa adding a further 1,600 kilometres. That this should have been so was hardly surprising, given what lay to hand. From Cape Town, the SAAF's locally assembled open-cockpit Wapitis lacked the range to patrol much beyond Hermanus or Saldanha Bay in occasional – and unconvincing – dawn and dusk practice-shows of shielding the approaches to Table Bay. The shipping approaches to Durban also relied on Hawker biplanes of severely limited range, in this case several barely serviceable 1931 Fury fighters.

Leaving aside these and about 50 Hawker Hartbees

ground support biplanes, which had been developed specially for South Africa in the mid-1930s, the SAAF possessed, in truth, no more than six modern machines – four Hawker Hurricane fighters and a couple of Bristol Blenheim and Fairey Battle light bombers. The latter were, in any case, a designer mistake. It was probably good fortune that Britain's Air Ministry did not lumber the minuscule SAAF with another recent folly, however symbolically appropriate it would have been as an addition to its arsenal. Named in honour of the country's first Prime Minister, General Louis Botha, it was the 1938 Blackburn Botha reconnaissance bomber, an underpowered contraption which was prone to fatal accidents.

Thrown on to its own meagre resources at the outset, the air force took the path of the army, that of snap improvisation. There, the General Staff had swiftly ordered the requisitioning of the country's Ford and Chevrolet motor assembly plants and secured large volumes of engines and spares from American suppliers, in order to forge a fully motorised brigade group for East Africa. In a similarly brisk adaptation to try to remedy constraints upon air striking power, the Defence Department elbowed SAA into the SAAF. That solution was to utilise converted SA Railways and Harbours workshops to turn out additional airframe components, so that the SAA's 18 twin-engined

Junkers JU-86 monoplanes could be equipped with gun turrets and bomb-racks. The small SAA fleet of wooden Airspeed Envoys also had their civilian life curtailed. Manufactured for colonial conditions and purpose-built for quick conversion by their British manufacturer, an Envoy required only thirty hours to be adapted to military use.

Next, there were South Africa's waters. Relying entirely on the British Navy as its guardian in grey, this big maritime country developed no passion for its own ships, leaving seaborne defences completely undeveloped. Unlike Australia and New Zealand, which possessed navies with cruisers, destroyers and purpose-built minesweepers, the Union had no warships at all. Astonishingly, the South African Naval Service (SANS) consisted of three officers and three ratings. Granted, there had not been complete complacency. In 1939 an attempt had been made to secure a First World War monitor warship, HMS *Erebus*, to provide heavy naval guns to stiffen the defences of Table Bay harbour. But the plan foundered when incessant squabbling among the South African crew sent out to take over the *Erebus* led a frosty Admiralty to reclaim the ship.

At the outbreak of war, the only sea-trained strength was the South African roll of the Royal Navy Volunteer Reserve (RNVR). A paltry 800 officers and ratings, this was in any event not a UDF contingent but under the command of the Admiralty's Africa Station at Simonstown. Trained on British ships and shepherded by a few retired RN officers who kept themselves salty, this local defence reserve had light seafaring and gunnery experience but was largely poorly prepared for the most obvious local naval demands – minesweeping and anti-submarine defence duties. With Defence Headquarters dominated by the concerns of the UDF's inland army and air force officers, the urgency of the problems of naval deficiency seemed to be little appreciated.

Elsewhere, though, by the beginning of September 1939 some thought was being given to what was about to happen. South Africa assigned trained sea gunners to 50 British merchant ships in its waters, and posted crewmen to several armed merchantmen, including Union Castle line mailships, which had been fitted out for defence in local ports by the Admiralty. And defence command was eyeing whatever could be pressed into service, which meant that it was poised to requisition vessels from local trawler and whaler fleets.

Meanwhile, the impending domestic civil situation was no less unsure, another shaky arena where the government could not sit on its haunches. In the early months of 1938, Oswald Pirow had already started to make provision for military deployment for the protection of key facilities and for the army to shore up police powers in the event of a national emergency. Such planning included the mobilisation of additional civil forces to secure vital industrial sectors and other strategically crucial resources, like harbours, against espionage and possible sabotage.

But if this cheered some who accepted the inevitability of war, it alienated a larger number of others who wanted no part of it. Thus, there were smouldering hostilities between the UDF and the police, which contained a disgruntled rump of anti-war Afrikaners, to which could be added divisions among policemen themselves over war preparations. The practical consequence was that very little was executed before the middle of 1939. Only then was the government able to implement its first Emergency Measures against sabotage, their jurisdiction imposed by a set of essential state agencies – the South African Police, the Board of Trade and Industries, and the Tender Board, and the Departments of Defence and of External Affairs. Just before Pretoria's declaration of war, these binding powers were used to cancel all police leave and in particular to prod the idling railway police into heightening its vigilance and raising its guard against the possible threat of sabotage.

In sharp contrast to military lethargy, there had been other solid anticipatory steps earlier in 1939. With national emergency in mind, in April the Department of Commerce and Industries had undertaken a thorough inventory of industrial and other vital resources, and had formulated enabling authority to impose official controls so as to conserve economic assets and check price inflation.

Several months later, a newly created National Supplies Control Board was empowered to play an extensive role in the control of national economic strategy. A thrusting administrative body which contained the Secretary for Defence, the Control Board assumed authority over a proliferation of things, including imports and exports, industrial raw materials, food, prices, rationing needs, the workforce of essential industries, and agricultural production and distribution. The scope, powers and competence of the Board as an effective national institution would grow rapidly during the war. Meanwhile, further Emergency Regulations were also being readied to marshal other critical economic sectors. Thus, the Union Treasury greatly extended the grip of its money controls. This enabled it to block any flight of capital, and also to direct all gold reserves and foreign exchange holdings to ensure that their primary use would be to pay for vital war goods and essential services from overseas, not only from Britain but also from countries like India, Australia, Canada and the United States.

Inevitably, there would be disruptions, examples

of bureaucratic bungling, instances of wastage and unplanned shortages, and misdirected efforts. But the overall effectiveness of the Union's late and scrambling efforts at economic mobilisation still stand out as a remarkable achievement under pressure. South Africa was able to adjust well to the imminent voraciousness of a war economy, limbering up for a heightened demand for goods and services of all kinds, especially those which would have to be supplied both to its own armed forces and to those of other Allied states.

In more than keeping itself afloat, the nature of that reorganisation and redirection would also come to reflect the classic shape of capitalist mobilisation for war. The wartime South African economy would remain capitalist in the fundamental sense of ruling market forces and the pursuit of profit. But the advent of conflict would also require substantial modifications of the market system, as its movements were too haphazard or too sluggish to respond to a national military push. The fashioning of some form of war or command economy would become inescapable, especially in priority sectors which would soon become embraced by rigorous planning and compulsion, from munitions manufacturing and aero engine assembly to food-canning lines and railways workshops. In much of its regulatory character, the organisation of the Union's war economy resembled that of America.

Of course, all of this hinged on the expectation of a great national exertion, rather than one of skirting the war as a bystander. And that, for a moment, was a far from open-and-shut case. We turn, now, to the joyless clash of views over where South Africa ought to have gone, and to the opening stage of the war in which the country landed.

4

Neutrality averted and early shadow-boxing

South Africa's war got off to a cracking start, with an early clear-cut victory. On 8 September, a German freighter, the *Hagen*, was still stuck in Durban harbour because of a dispute over handling fees. It was a sitting target for an intrepid Major Beyers, who boarded the enemy ship with an armed railways police detachment and took its crew prisoner. With the press lined up, the Hamburg merchant seamen were conducted ashore by Beyers and his boarders and shunted off into internment. Roped away as enemy aliens, they would be joined in camps by local Italians, transient Vichy French seamen and an assortment of the usual South African suspects, numbering almost 4,000 by August 1940. The acting port captain, Captain H.G. Jarvis, made the most of running down the Swastika and attaching the *Hagen* as the Union's first prize of war.

Five days earlier, the Union Cabinet had had its

own kind of theatrical warfare between parliamentary generals and their brooding courtiers, set on going one of two ways. The post-1934 Fusion government or coalition United South African National Party government was at loggerheads over what to do about the war. Six ministers, including the Prime Minister, J.B.M. Hertzog, and Oswald Pirow, argued for remaining neutral and for upholding national sovereignty, apart from discharging the legal requirement to protect Britain's Simonstown facility. Without neutrality, rumbled General J.C.G. Kemp, there would be 'a bloodbath in South Africa'. Seven other Cabinet members, prominent among whom were Smuts, the Deputy Prime Minister, and his long-time ally Deneys Reitz, pushed for joining the war against Germany as a matter of duty, national interest and security. It is recorded that this final, fractured Cabinet gathering ended with sherry, but not whether it was sweet or dry.

On 4 September, the position was resolved in a tense and impassioned parliamentary exchange in which the crusty generals drew their battle lines. In essence, Hertzog's Nationalist position was that South Africa had no interest in a war between Germany and Poland, nor in contributing to a war that was being waged by a wronged Germany to avenge its old humiliation at Versailles. On the other hand, for the Union to throw in its lot with Britain and its empire would be insufferable, as the only white citizens who desired this were those whose loyalty lay more with London than with Pretoria. Only through neutrality could South Africa preserve its full national independence and the freedom to chart its own destiny. A gut conviction, it was expressed soberly and powerfully.

It cut no ice with the United Party's Smuts. Hitler was bent on world domination, and Germany would assuredly demand the return of South West Africa. Were that to have to be relinquished, western border security would be gone and there would be an open door into the Union. On its own, South Africa's chances of survival were slight. By cutting loose from its British Commonwealth friends and allies, it would find itself adrift and alone in an increasingly perilous world.

In a parliamentary division, General Hertzog's neutrality motion was defeated by 80 votes to 67, and Smuts got his political mandate for war on 6 September. It was less than resounding, his case probably having been carried in part because of its shrewd (but bogus) assurance that the government 'should not send forces overseas as in the last war'. Reconciling the fiercely irreconcilable then had a bad start, courtesy of the Union's relieved Governor-General, Sir Patrick Duncan, who delivered the formal declaration of a state of war with Germany, 'in the name of His Majesty the King'.

As if rubbing in more salt, Duncan had turned a deaf ear to clamour from the Hertzog camp that he call a general election on the controversial issue of war entry. Defeated by his coalition deputy, Hertzog resigned the premiership and joined D.F. Malan's more hydraulic Afrikaner nationalists in opposition. With his parliamentary position bolstered by the fringe pro-war Labour and Dominion parties, Smuts as the new Prime Minister was authorised by the Governor-General to form a fresh coalition war government. Anything but clear-cut, the move to war would not be on the usual basis of a bipartisan parliamentary consensus in which all members stood behind those fighting in support of the country.

The attitudes of those outside parliament were also mixed. To be sure, within the ranks of a gushing pro-war minority, press editorials and correspondence hailed a decisive end to the uncertainties and divisions of the early spring. A right-thinking General Smuts had ushered in a sense of purpose and unity. For the romanticising *Cape Times* and *The Star* in 1939 and 1940, the soldiering Springboks of the UDF would inherently be the best troops for the demands of modern warfare. Not only were they educated, skilled, adaptable and nimble. Born of the veldt, their lengthy colonial fighting pedigree fitted them for any terrain, as had been demonstrated through African desert and bush and European mud during 1914–18. In this celebration of martial masculinity, South Africans were itching to saddle up, to *opsaal*, for any theatre of war in the world. In 1939 they were up there with the Australians as southern Africa's white Gurkhas of the Empire, ready to carry a fight 'Up North', in that grammatical touchstone of patriotic volunteer identity in the 1940s.

Nor were such men all white and English. Another revered strain was that of robust and high-minded Afrikaner patriots who carried within them the seed of the Boer combat tradition, long on endurance, initiative and sharpshooting. In one November 1939 editorial, the *Diamond Fields Advertiser* conjured up something of the novelistic *Thirty-Nine Steps* and *Greenmantle* aura of Buchan. In this depiction, the rallying of some or other element of the virtuous 'stout Afrikander', such as the pilot warrior Piet, came to the defence of Empire, helping to rescue civilisation from collapse.

Behind – or, more accurately perhaps, below – these images of vaulting white war patriots came the assurance of African loyalism. For Alan Paton, then head of a Johannesburg reformatory for African youths, it was an uplifting moment of pulling together. In his autobiographical *Towards the Mountain* (1980), he recalled convening a white staff meeting on one of the early days of the war. Although 'many white South Africans' were gripped by 'a kind of crusading spirit', the surliness of the 'anti-war brigade' constituted by his own largely Afrikaner staff left him exasperated and pessimistic. It remained for the black staff and their 'unanimous support' for 'the vigorous prosecution of the war' to lift Paton's spirits.

At a separate gathering of African staff, he found 'no hostility at all'. After all, 'it was well known that Hitler regarded black people as inferior creatures, fit only to obey'. Some of those assembled, he reasoned, 'would have asked permission to enlist', only for front-line hopes to have been dashed, for 'in South Africa a black man might not bear arms'. Yet to Africans still went the badge of patient and honourable conduct. Reconciled to their war role, the 'black contribution would be harder work' on a bigger scale, involving 'longer hours'. That effort, Alan Paton concluded fondly, 'they were fully prepared to make'.

Other views – of a more pervasive sort – were very different or even exactly the reverse. In Paton's own native Natal, there was little stomach for war from the liberally inclined *Witness*, whose editor, George Galpin, had been left with pacifist instincts by his Quaker upbringing. The *Natal Witness* had applauded Neville Chamberlain's 1938 Munich agreement with Hitler, and regarded the war as too barbarous a burden to be borne. It was not to be its only denunciation. In one of its polemics of the early 1940s, the paper reflected that in its anti-Fascist war the Union ought to have been more mindful of the state of its own backyard. There, it alleged, the grim compound conditions of migrant labourers on some Witwatersrand gold mines resembled those of Nazi concentration camps.

To be anti-war in South African society – either at the start of the conflict or for its entire duration – was to be a member of an exceptionally broad church. Naturally, the Union had its little knots of Quakers, anti-militarist socialists, war-hating liberals and non-violent Christians, but these came nowhere close to resembling the campaigning anti-war constituencies of Europe, especially in Britain. Those in South Africa who were against war opposed it in their own local ways, based as much on their own old grievances as on any body of common beliefs.

Therefore, as the East London *Daily Dispatch* observed in December 1939, among Africans there was 'no appetite for the present war', but instead 'apathy'. The reason was that they were 'wholly unconvinced of the truth of the causes and aims of this present war', and realised 'that they as an oppressed people do not count anywhere in its aims'. One expression of that mood was a cynicism about the fruits of yet another undertaking for imperial Britain. 'Why', snapped a writer in *Imvo Zabantsundu* in January 1940, 'should we fight for you? We fought for you in the Boer War, and you left us to the Dutch. We also fought for you in the last war. Our lives were sacrificed for you in France as well as in East Africa. When that time was over, did anyone care about our future ... was there ever concern about us? Truly, what have we to fight for?'

This was mostly what parliamentary liberal white Native Representatives found when doing their political milk rounds in rural districts. When trying to interest Africans in the conflict, they ran into a wall of apathy. If all this was discouraging, it was also, in the view of Britain's High Commissioner, understandable. Reporting to Clement Attlee, Dominions Secretary in Churchill's post-1940 government, Lord Harlech advised that much African enthusiasm for the 'democratic cause' was scarcely to be expected, given that it had 'yielded' them 'so little in the way of material benefits'.

Disillusionment could also take other, more extreme directions. During the Great War, chafing Johannesburg African mineworkers and deprived Zulu and Xhosa communities along the south-eastern coast who associated English mine-owners and land-owners with squalid working conditions and landlessness had looked to a German landing as an emancipation. It was not for nothing that, early in 1915, Chief Mhlohlo

Mvuso Matanzima Mtirara of the Transkei had named his new-born son Kaiser. So it was to be with Germany, again, in late 1939 and early 1940, and later with a major alarm over rumours of a Japanese invasion in 1942.

As intelligence reports and some press observers noted, among restive groups of Africans the war was feeding millenarian hopes stuffed with hazy fantasies of the fall of the Union, after which lost lands and prosperity might be restored by a conquering enemy likely to be well disposed towards the country's underdogs. Here, there was no dread of war, more a mentality of subversive expectation, with some alienated Africans known to be cheering on 'the military gains of the German Reich ... unhappily the nature of this present struggle is not well understood ... this is simply an emotional alliance with whoever happens to be the enemy of South Africa.'

Equally, such disloyal impulses were not confined to South Africa. Following the surrender of France, British Home intelligence agents monitoring morale in cafés and bars picked up murmurings among discontented workers that a Hitler victory might not be so bad a thing after all, as the German target would be 'the bosses'.

The Union's segregationist order also provided irony for left-wing critics in bodies such as the mainly

Coloured Non-European United Front (NEUF) to scorn the local brand of *herrenvolk* (master race) democracy, and to expose the hollowness of its claims to be joining a struggle to preserve rights and freedoms. From elsewhere on the political margins, the African National Congress (ANC), too, registered its dissent. A resolution of its December 1939 conference declared that 'unless the government grants the Africans full democratic and citizenship rights', the ANC was 'not prepared to advise the Africans to participate in the present war, in any capacity'. It was serving the national war effort on equal terms with whites, including the bearing of arms, or no war at all. A blunt opening stand, it was, however, one on which the organisation's leadership would later soften in its overarching support of the British and Allied cause.

The tiny Communist Party of South Africa (CPSA) came to its anti-war conclusion after confused debate over what to do about the menace of Fascism. In due course, it toed the orthodox line laid down following the August 1939 Hitler–Soviet Pact in which the international communist movement defined the war as an inter-imperialist clash and against the interests of workers. CPSA members such as Yusuf Dadoo joined Indian compatriots like Ahmed Kathrada of the NEUF in a campaign against war-making in 1939 and 1940.

Swayed by the anti-colonial and anti-British

polemics of the Indian nationalist movement, Dadoo mocked appeals to the black majority to enlist in a war for freedom, justice and democracy. Addressing that audience, he asked, rhetorically, whether they enjoyed 'the fruits of freedom, justice and democracy', before providing the answer. Theirs was the enjoyment of 'the pass and poll tax laws, segregation, and white labour policy ... low wages, high rents, poverty, unemployment and vicious colour bar laws.' The party also debunked enlistment by African volunteers as unarmed auxiliary soldiers. Its insulting line was that such men had learned nothing from the service experience of 1914–18, in which they had been the gullible dupes of European imperialism, the cooking and cleaning 'boy' servants of white masters, and so farcically emasculated that they were not soldiering men.

Meanwhile, in parliament, flintier Afrikaner nationalists were feeling as buoyed by Hitler's movements as they had been by the spectacle of the 1938 Great Trek centenary celebrations. With the war opening so well for Berlin, these months were a honeymoon with Hitler. What united those who were professedly pro-German with those who, like many Irish republicans, were simply anti-British was a shared desire to see England get it in the neck, even an intoxication with the idea of a British defeat. Thus, in the House of Assembly in May 1940, shortly before the start of the Battle of Britain, one Nationalist MP declared it 'right' that the people of Britain should have their homes incinerated. Then, they could realise at last what Afrikaners had suffered in their lost War of Independence. At a party congress several months later, B.J. Schoeman (after 1948, Minister of Labour and then of Transport) went further, welcoming a German victory as it would speed things up. 'The whole future of Afrikanerdom', he asserted, was 'dependent on a German victory' for, if it won the war, 'we shall be able to negotiate with her, and in that way ensure the establishment of an independent republic in South Africa'.

In this atmosphere, with the air clouded by daily scares about espionage, sabotage, fifth columns and invasion fears, the Smuts government had to tread warily. On a tightrope politically, it had to press ahead to get an unprepared and mostly unwilling country prepared for war. For that, it needed a steadying pole. Having said more than once that the Union was finding itself fighting a war on two fronts, the Prime Minister's public political gestures were often studiously pious. Accordingly, the tone of his first wartime New Year's Eve radio address, delivered in English, was more balm than bellicosity. It was 'bad luck' to have fallen into the 'calamity' of 'another great war'. Nevertheless, with 'heaven's high blessing', the year ahead might well still see hostilities resolved by a 'fruitful peace' from which 'the frail bark of our western civilisation may unexpectedly sail out of the storm into smooth waters'.

The inescapable 'sadder side' of national life was continuing political fractiousness. 'People do not seem to have realised yet', Smuts continued, 'that this country is really at war.' How else could it be that 'instead of uniting round our leadership', they were decrying it? Yet, like it or not, war was 'no longer an open or debatable question ... as if the rights and wrongs of our being at war' could 'still be debated as an open question'. For 'that issue' had been 'decided and closed', and it was now up to 'every patriotic South African' to make the 'well-being of his country' an absolute priority.

In underlining its importance, Smuts could not resist a classical conceit, reminding his listeners of the 'ancient war formula of the Roman Senate'. The 'first duty' of 'all our political leaders of whatever party' was to heed 'the consuls', who had declared that 'no harm befalls the state'. That meant having to 'put our house in order in so short a time', a task being shouldered 'right nobly' by 'the young manhood of South Africa'.

The Prime Minister left a challenge of another sort to the end, the fretful question of 'choice' and its bearing upon 'specifically ... my Afrikaans-speaking friends and all parties involved'. 'That choice', Smuts recognised, 'was relatively easy for the English-speaking Afrikaners to make', for, naturally, 'their hearts agreed with their heads'. However, 'for Dutch Afrikaners the choice was a crisis which hit deep', leaving the wound of 'tragic division among us'. Yet do not, he pleaded, 'allow the crisis to become a tragedy' by springing from division into an unreasonably fixed judgement.

Rather oddly for a message aimed at anti-British Afrikaners, Smuts then rounded off with the historically tricky figure of Oliver Cromwell. Granted, Cromwell was a reassuringly Protestant and puritanical character upon whom to draw. He was, though, also the colonial English conqueror of Ireland in the seventeenth century. Heed the lesson of Cromwell's words, Smuts urged, in which 'even the bitterest opponents concede that it may be possible for them to be wrong'. An unintentional poke in the eye, it was unlikely to bring discontented nationalists around to following the wisdom of Smuts and Cromwell. For that matter, it was probably also just as well that so few Afrikaners were Catholic. As Smuts had set out to show, it was possible to love both English and Afrikaners. But they were loves of a different kind.

While the presence of the war was growing in the new year, it was not by leaps and bounds. Few white combat recruits were joining the reedy lines of volunteers at Command depots – on the

Witwatersrand, for example, in the early part of 1940 it was merely several hundred men a day. In this phase, it was as well that the weight of the war remained away from the door. Indeed, for the better part of its first two years it was, if anything, shadow-boxing, an almost impalpable engagement for most inhabitants. Life's daily rhythms rolled on, although postage stamps had soon to shrink in size because of paper shortages. And early in the 1940s wedding-cake makers were upset by the introduction of restrictions on the use of white flour. One major domestic sacrifice asked of better-off white and other middle-class households was that they not 'keep more servants' than they 'really required', thereby releasing black labour 'for more useful' war-related work.

It was only later that the Union began to feel a pinch. Following Japan's entry into the war in 1941 and its swift Far Eastern territorial conquests, some local import sources and supply routes were hit. Stocks ran down, shipping volumes contracted and petrol rationing was introduced. The government also appointed a Food Controller and brought in price and import controls. Even so, in comparison with a straitened Europe, the Union was not a place of queues for powdered eggs. Whatever it was that defined the war for its inhabitants, it was not the ration book. British child evacuees shipped to the protection of Johannesburg and Kimberley never stopped marvelling at the well-stocked larders of the homes which took them in, and at what shop shelves continued to carry. Of course, destitute African agriculturalists and unemployed and impoverished urban communities did not enjoy wartime food security. But shortages were sufficiently bearable not to become a contentious public political problem. Nor did Allied supply demands drain away needed commodities, something which would have aggravated anti-war sentiment.

All the same, the first two years or so of hostilities were still crammed with fearfulness and uncertainty over various vulnerable danger-spots. Just a few years earlier, in 1936, Hertzog had already fingered Abyssinia and Italy's next steps there as a future worry for southern African security. Three years later, Italian concerns were still at the top, with Smuts and the government of Southern Rhodesia sharing an immediate concern over protection of the southern frontiers of British East Africa. Drawing up to hold the line at the Limpopo River was regarded as a bridge too close.

So, getting ahead of himself as usual, on 7 September Smuts proposed to London that a Union infantry brigade and 'several' air squadrons be pushed up as a precautionary reinforcement of Kenya. It was a good thing that Britain did not take the bait. For, with neither the brigade readiness nor the squadrons at his disposal, Smuts had nothing to send. In effect, his face was saved by Chamberlain's Dominions Secretary, Anthony Eden, who was anxious not to trigger any African trouble prematurely. Whitehall, Smuts was reassured, did not consider Kenya to be under threat and was anxious not to do anything that might provoke Rome.

At this stage, Smuts was taking the realistic view that it was only a matter of time before Italy became a belligerent, whatever Mussolini's cagey initial show of non-belligerence. South Africa's preparations for that eventuality would also have to form part of a wider strategic African calculation. Its southernmost location at the eastern and western oceanic junction meant that it could not avoid getting sucked into a wider world conflict. Not only was war in Africa a certainty, as a fighting Italy would be assured by Germany of pickings in North Africa and in the Mediterranean. In the event of Tokyo being drawn in, there was the further possibility of a Japanese strike from the east at South African ports.

Some of this apprehension focused on a bombing war from the air, a once far-fetched prospect that was then beginning to look suddenly less far-fetched. With a combined air strength in Libya and in East Africa of several hundred long-range bombers, recently battle-tested in Spain and in Abyssinia, Italy appeared to have the technical means for attacks on Transvaal urban centres and strategically tempting industrial sectors. Ominously, its air force, the Regia Aeronautica, had medium bombers like the Cant Z 1007b with a reach of some 2,500 kilometres. This made the mines and factories of the Witwatersrand an attainable target from Tanganyika, the Belgian Congo, Mozambique and Angola, or even Madagascar. Still starved of speedy monoplane fighters, the SAAF had scant hope of being a deterrent. However unfounded, perceptions of Italian air strength stirred things up, with the *Rand Daily Mail* in November 1939 reminding readers of Mussolini's fearsome prewar boast of possessing almost 9,000 aircraft, sufficient to blot out the sun. (With fewer than one-tenth of that total, the claim was ludicrous.) It was enough to galvanise some leafier Johannesburg households into constructing air-raid shelters in their gardens.

On top of having to contend immediately with German U-boats, larger Italian submarines with a long patrolling capability also featured as a potential threat, with Rome's small underwater fleet at Massawa on the Red Sea coast poised to menace shipping off Durban and along the Mozambique Channel. A submarine offensive against the northward flow of shipping from local waters posed a serious problem – for Britain's communications with India and the Far East, for the movement of Middle East oil supplies, and for the transportation of forces, reinforcements and supplies that would be needed to take on an Italian adversary in Africa and the Middle East.

However alarmist and exaggerated in scale such fears may have been, they reflected feverish days, high on uncertainty and on the smell of danger and confrontation. It was also not all excitable nonsense. Soon after war got under way, German submarines, surface raiders and mines were endangering the Cape sea-route; later, Italian and Japanese submarines added to the threat. In the course of hostilities, over 150 merchant ships amounting to almost 890,000 gross tons were sunk within a wide radius of the South African and South West African coasts, for the loss of merely three enemy submarines.

With the need for secrecy over ships and routes an imperative, the censorship net around major ports was cast widely. Appealing to coastal inhabitants to keep their mouths shut, an RN Rear-Admiral at Simonstown informed the curious in 1942 that naturally it required 'some self-restraint' to 'refrain from telling your friends and starting an ever-widening ripple of gossip' about your sighting of a naval ship or a 'large convoy' or an 'interesting merchant vessel' which had berthed. But such sensitive information could reach the enemy.

Britannia in the Bay: HMS Ark Royal *in Cape Town harbour. (National Library of SA, Cape Town)*

Accordingly, should you 'see a ship lying at anchor from Table Mountain or the Bluff at Durban, don't pass it on. Do what Nelson did. Turn a blind eye and forget that you've seen it.'

More distant and malign observers also became an early obsession. With convoy traffic sailing up the south-east African coast, Portuguese East Africa could not fail to attract a beady eye. Linked in the imagination of the Admiralty to the prospective new front of a stealthy 'Asiatic war', Mozambique was recognised to be a teeming hive of international intrigue among German, Italian, British and even American agents. Malcolm Muggeridge, then a fake British vice-consul immersed in secret assignments in Lourenço Marques, shared South African suspicions of what the German and Italian consuls-general were up to. The latter was regarded as the more dangerous plotter, assumed to be jotting down shipping information for transmission to lurking submarine commanders. South African agents stationed in the suspect Portuguese territory were also alert to a possible Italian or German diversionary move on the Union through Lourenço Marques.

Early in 1940, their intelligence estimates put the number of German residents at the port at 2,000, and up to no good. They were reportedly involved in laying out a large airfield, to be addicted to organised open-air activities more military than recreational in tone, and were also rumoured to be training Africans for who knew what. In the first week of June 1940, a few days before the collapse of France and Italy's war declaration, Sir Pierre van Ryneveld, the UDF Chief of the General Staff, moved army detachments to a Komatipoort border position and placed troop-carrying aircraft and bombers on immediate readiness for a possible incursion into Mozambique.

This was, in fact, only part of that little story. For the Union had also crafted its Z Plan, a lightning campaign scheme which was kept under wraps well into the postwar decades for fear of treading on Portuguese diplomatic corns. A contingency for an invasion of Mozambique and the occupation of Lourenço Marques, the Z blueprint had been compiled by Brigadier-General George Brink, before he was given command of the 1st SA Division for deployment in East Africa. Its basis was provided by the need to dish the enemy in Lourenço Marques should it pose too great a danger. A pure, no-nonsense soldier when given his head, Brink envisaged the deployment of a motorised infantry brigade with armoured cars and air support to punch through the Portuguese territory and seize its key port before the local Germans could get out of bed. Never more than an idea, it was, you might say, the South African *blitzkrieg* that never was.

Jitters about Lisbon's colony serving as an enemy landing-ground on the doorstep subsided eventually, just as surveillance diminished of scrap-metal dealers in Lourenço Marques, as well as in Walvis Bay, who were suspected of stockpiling secretly to leap to the supply needs of enemy raiders. Still, Pretoria kept up its guard. In 1943, the border with Portuguese East Africa was made a prohibited area and the UDF posted auxiliary home defence African guards along its entire length to curb crossings by enemy agents and to block the flow of sensitive information.

Earlier, there had been a different passing alarm to the west. A security worry in the months leading up to war was what a nest of local Nazis, put at several hundred, might get up to in a lightly held South West Africa, such as storming the Walvis Bay radio station to stage a *putsch.* Any rash impulses were quickly checked by the precautionary drafting in of SA Police reinforcements. But episodic fears of enemy probing of the softness of the territory's lengthy coastline persisted into the early 1940s, with the SAAF coastal wing running close search sweeps for hidden German submarine lairs right up to the Kunene River mouth on the Angolan border. All the while, the Smuts administration was also having to pay heed to unsettled domestic security circumstances, our next consideration.

The Lady in White

In chilling rural superstitions, a white lady or a lady in white usually refers to a female ghost, frequently that of a haunting nun. Although often associated with popular medieval and Victorian British legend, tall tales of milky white ladies clad in flowing white dresses are a world-wide phenomenon. In South Africa, the war produced a completely different kind of white lady, a plump, matronly character who set out to warm and not freeze the blood of men. As recorded vividly in June 1942 by *Dover Sole*, a British troopship flysheet, when the vessel pulled away from its berth for its onward voyage to India, 'at the end of the jetty that white-clad figure started singing *Auld Lang Syne*. As the gap grew, just snatches of the words came to us, and finally, just a picture of that solitary figure in white waving to us, and we swear she was still singing. We may forget many things of this war, but never the songs of Durban's lady in white.' Associated indelibly with South Africa's war experience, the Lady in White was, in a way, a kind of traditional ship's female figurehead, a maternal bringer of luck even if on the shore. Born in 1891, this singer was Perla Siedle. The daughter of a wealthy local ship-owning family, Siedle had studied opera in Germany as a young woman, becoming an able Wagnerian soprano who gave recitals in London, Vienna and New York. Her 'wharfside' soprano turns started in 1940, according to an interview given to New York's *Life* Magazine in December 1943. In that year, as Siedle (also known as Perla or Paula Gibson) was waving off a passing Irish sailor who had been looked after by her family, he apparently shouted a request to her across the water to sing 'something Irish'. Instinctively, through cupped hands she obliged with *When Irish Eyes Are Smiling*. Wearing her trademark billowing white dress, bright red felt or straw hat and sturdy beige shoes, the smiling Perla Siedle became a fixture of Durban harbour by the mid-1940s. With a husband who went on to serve in Italy and two sons and a daughter in the army, she regarded the Durban quays as her own war station or posting, and her troopship entertaining as work. Her soaring soprano tones amplified by a megaphone salvaged from a torpedoed ship by British sailors, Siedle reputedly sang to over 5,000 ships conveying more than a quarter of a million Allied servicemen. Troops in transit and the public lapped her up as an extraordinary morale-boosting figure, a dignified and homely crooner whose wide repertoire underlined South Africa's place as an international crossroads. Also known to some as Ma or Nightingale, the Lady in White provided *Sarie Marais* for the UDF, opera arias for Poles, Czechs and Greeks, *Waltzing Matilda* for Australians, *The Star-Spangled Banner* for American GIs, and *There'll Always Be an England* for British soldiers. Managing to be both stirring and sentimental, Perla Siedle became an Allied celebrity, another 'forces' sweetheart' like Vera Lynn, if more maternal than romantic. With a voice of the sea-waves rather than the air-waves, she was saluted not only by soldiers and sailors but also by all manner of ships, with captains sounding horns or bells as their vessels slid past her on the quayside.

5

Not fighting on the beaches

However much it may have ground into the psyche of the country, a viable enemy invasion from across land or from the sea was always a very far-fetched eventuality. Nor did the Union have to see it all the way through on tenterhooks. From the end of 1943 coastal vigilance eased and, aside from Civic Guard protection of key installations like harbour oil stores, all invasion watch operations by the Civilian Protective Services were suspended beyond 30 kilometres of the coast. By then, there was also no further need to be busied by Italy, following its agreement to an Anglo-American armistice in the second half of that year. Although its 60,000 prisoners of war, bagged mainly in the East African and North African campaigns, continued to be cooped up, Italian residents were no longer restricted. A more relaxing time had come, one in which to worry less about the dangers of the foreign enemy.

A far greater nuisance than this, if also for a

similar time, was posed by far-right Afrikaner anti-war radicalism. Its intrusiveness obliged the Smuts government to steer its war policies with considerable caution, and to pursue some mobilisation practices that might otherwise have been rather more sweeping. Thus, as in the First World War, there was no question of introducing white conscription, of bringing the Union's European nation and army together to forge the customary masculine ideal of a nation-in-arms. As armed duty and patriotic sacrifice were not the universally accepted obligations of citizenship in 1939, it mattered profoundly whether forces were to be volunteer or conscript. Fittingly, Oswald Pirow sounded an early Nationalist warning in 1939, threatening opposition to *any* dispatch of *existing* troops beyond the borders of the Union. With the tense political balance within the white population too delicate to be resolved by any wholesale commandeering, Pretoria had to be wary of plunging in too deeply.

Organised anti-war hostilities coursed through two main channels, linked gingerly at first before parting into their own political worlds of parliamentary respectability and extra-parliamentary, paramilitary strutting. Constitutional Afrikaner opposition was mounted by the combined Nationalists, with a faction of Hertzog's old National Party and D.F. Malan's Purified National Party making up the official

Opposition. Differing from Hertzog's brand of earnest neutrality and his belief in a shared Afrikaner-Anglo order based on a common primary loyalty to South Africa, Malan's wartime position was unambiguously pro-German, anti-British and committed to the realisation of Afrikaner nationalist domination of political life. Too shrewd and too fastidious to fall for street extremism, though, he kept his feet squarely under parliamentary benches. Uneven political tastes and long-standing personal animosity between Malan and a fading Hertzog ensured that unity did not last long. In 1940, the ex-Prime Minister broke with the Malan camp and left public life, a victim of the homelessness which the war had created.

The other side of the coin of disaffection was explicitly non-parliamentary. Favouring the Nazi German cause more than actual neutrality, this highly vocal anti-war constituency included students and other younger people who were disgusted by the pro-war outcome in parliament. For *Besembos*, the university student journal in Potchefstroom, it meant that South Africa 'must wage war against a people with which the Afrikaner nation has no other relationship than that of friendship', in support of England, 'our only foreign enemy'. Radical agitation gravitated sharply towards authoritarian extra-parliamentary movements, most notably the large and, initially at least, successful Ossewabrandwag (Ox-wagon sentinel, or OB).

Spawned by the mass commemorative tide of the 1938 Afrikaner Great Trek centennial, the OB had been launched early in 1939 as a cultural body with a fairly elastic definition of culture. It was organised on a commando basis under a *kommandant-generaal*, Colonel J.C. Laas, a farmer and part-time UDF soldier. Male followers had a love of beards, corduroy and mounted saddles, while the long Voortrekker dresses of female members pointed in the same nineteenth-century direction. Wrapped up in a nostalgic dream of the re-establishment of an independent Afrikaner republic, a pining OB devoted its energies to the healthy pursuits of drill, camps, muscular folk sports and regular rifle practice. The Hertzog government did not find this quaint. Before peace ended, Laas was dismissed from the UDF and its serving officers were forbidden to join the movement.

Concerned little with the Union's own racial policies, the OB cultivated open admiration of German National Socialism and the push for ethnic purity. Its ideological armoury reflected anti-Semitism as well as a consuming fear of what Kowie Marais, Afrikaans programme head at the SABC early in 1940 (and much later a Progressive Party MP), identified as 'communist-socialist' trends within the Allied cause.

Not dressed for the boxing ring: Robey Leibbrandt on his release from jail. (National Library of SA, Cape Town)

Influenced by the booted style of German Fascism, the OB came to embody not only a frustrated rejection of parliamentary politics, but a belief in its own national patriotic alternative.

This was dreamy faith in a paramilitary mobilisation to topple the government and bring on a corporate nationalist Afrikaner order that could seize power in conjunction with a final German victory in Europe. The solvent of British economic, cultural and other influences in South African life would be Germanic. And in doing what could be done to water the ground, non-parliamentary militancy was the mother of invention. This was certainly how it was seen by Laas's successor, Johannes (Hans) van Rensburg. Giving his tepid views on constitutionality, Van Rensburg, who resigned from his position as Administrator of the Orange Free State to take up the OB leadership early in 1941, concluded, 'if I have to choose between Afrikanerdom and democracy there is no choice ... I am not in the least concerned about the system.'

Naturally, Germany contrived to feed this fervour. For some years, Berlin's short-wave external broadcasting station, Radio Zeesen, the first in the world to transmit internationally and regularly in Afrikaans, had been beaming Nazi propaganda to southern Africa. Roused, the British Broadcasting Corporation (BBC) commenced its own counter-propaganda Afrikaans-language broadcasts from 1937. With war under way, Radio Zeesen increased its transmission hours and expanded its daily microphone ration of stories. Delivered by the dour figure of Erik Holm, a former Natal school headmaster, reports of a crippled Britain joined lurid accounts of Anglo-Boer War atrocities and denunciations of Jewish capitalist exploitation of Afrikaner workers.

More sensationalist, yet ultimately nothing more than a damp squib, was the bizarre plot involving the burly ex-Springbok pugilist Robey Leibbrandt. He was a tailor-made catalyst for Operation Weissdorn, a plot hatched by Admiral Wilhelm Canaris, head of the Abwehr, the German military intelligence service, to eliminate Smuts and force through a coup d'état by harnessing the subversive potential of the OB. Under the code name of Walter Kempf, Leibbrandt was to be secreted back to South Africa to intercede with Van Rensburg and have the OB readied.

In June 1941, carting 10,000 US dollars and a wireless transmitter with which to communicate with Berlin, a sea-sick Leibbrandt was put ashore on his own off a dark Namaqualand coast from a Vichy French yacht under German command. Although his dinghy capsized, his luck held and he made land. That was certainly more than could be said of another of Canaris's Abwehr agents, the Irish Republican Army leader Seán Russell. Also a former boxer and weight-lifter, Russell was to have been landed on Ireland's Dingle Peninsula in Operation Dove, almost a carbon copy of the half-Irish Leibbrandt's clandestine undertaking. There, the IRA man was to have created mischief in Ireland to coincide with the German invasion of Britain. Cursed, like Leibbrandt, with poor sea-legs, the hapless Russell's vomiting and stomach cramps grew so acute that he died before landing. Both were Nazi agents propelled by comparably outlandish schemes, an uncanny real-life version of the famous Erskine Childers nautical thriller, *The Riddle of the Sands* (1903), with its high drama of secret German invasion plots, yachts through the fog, and renegade masterminds.

Whereas the IRA Chief of Staff died sordidly aboard a U-boat, Leibbrandt would survive the Atlantic and more besides, living into the 1960s as a butcher in the north-western Cape and the author of crank political pamphlets. In seeking to galvanise extreme anti-Smuts forces, his reach exceeded his grasp. Darting about for a while, he made overtures to the OB but got nowhere with a disdainful Van Rensburg, for whom he was just too much to put up with. Unable to resist the personal urge for fiery leadership, Leibbrandt then proceeded to form his own entourage of national socialist rebels, stumping through the Orange Free State and the Transvaal to gain converts. He had, in Evelyn Waugh's memorable judgement in *Waugh in Abyssinia* (1936), the 'fatal' flaw 'of minor fascists', too much 'love of oratory'.

After taking a chilling blood oath, Leibbrandt's recruits trained as saboteurs, making time bombs and planning raids on banks and explosive dumps. Rumbled before managing anything very serious, the armed Abwehr plant went on the run but was cornered in Pretoria where he was arrested by a police sergeant who happened to be yet another former Springbok boxer. It was the end of Robey Leibbrandt's ring in more ways than one. In 1943 he was found guilty of high treason or, as the *Rand Daily Mail* reported on 11 March, of wielding 'the sword of Adolf Hitler' for a 'national socialist South Africa'. It had been an ineffectual rush, if more of blood and soil than blood and canvas.

Smuts intervened with clemency, commuting Leibbrandt's death sentence to life imprisonment. As many might have anticipated, the Prime Minister was keen not to turn him into a rebel martyr, as had happened with Jopie Fourie in the First World War Afrikaner Rebellion. Those times, too, had, in any event, also changed. By 1939, the loyalty of the army's generals could be counted on. That aside, the government was not, as in 1914, to be caught napping at the start of hostilities. With the opening of the first detention camp at Baviaanspoort in mid-September 1939, emergency regulations allowed for the summary internment of identified arch-troublemakers, action followed not long after by the impounding of firearms.

At the same time, to avoid making a contentious issue more contentious, the authorities steered clear of banning extremist anti-war organisations. The paradox of wartime security was that it kept South Africa both unfree and free. For a few thousand hotheads who were going too far, their war was ended by a plainclothes swoop and internment. Otherwise, hundreds of thousands of ordinary OB members could dream aloud, hold forth, and write and shout away without fear of being arrested or often even of being listened to.

Certainly, it was possible to make light of many of the protests by OB adherents and other heart-on-their sleeve dissidents, as these were minor acts of personal truculence. Stony Dutch Reformed Church *dominees* refused to marry Afrikaner servicemen or baptise their children. Others were barred from attending DRC services in uniform to avoid offending anti-war congregations. In the case of civil servants, Paton's *Towards the Mountain* is again vivid. Following the 1940 ban on police membership of the OB, government employees were barred from sporting its badge. The response of Paton's staff was to substitute mineral water bottle caps in their buttonholes. As their only act of war, it was on the scale of Lady Throbbing removing the portrait of the Kaiser from the menservants' lavatory in 1914, in Waugh's satirical novel *Vile Bodies* (1930). Because of so much posturing or, possibly, despite it, the OB became more an umbrella under which the most radical anti-war elements could congregate than the properly regimented basis of a concerted insurrection. This conflict, unlike the Great War, would not touch off an Afrikaner rebellion, even one with the life of a comet.

Nonetheless, the OB still became a mass focus of extreme nationalist anti-war activity. By the end of

1940, the stage at which the government had managed to dredge up 137,000 men under arms, the OB claimed the loyalty of twice that number, with a membership of some 400,000 at the peak of its exertions. Varying independent measures of OB strength were equally substantial, estimating a following of between 250,000 and 400,000 when it was at full cry. Even Durban, second to none in its fondness for the Union Jack, had 4,000 members. Inevitably, the overblown quality of the OB turned it into a Frankenstein's monster for more respectable nationalists. The truth is, Malan's Nationalists and the Ossewabrandwag may have been united in their opposition to the country's war effort, but not in the OB's extremism.

While Malan and Van Rensburg both believed that political prospects turned on the outcome of the war, the former looked to a resolution through diplomatic negotiations with Germany, while the latter was all for the adventurism of a popular mobilisation, its route to republican freedom fuelled by wartime crisis. It was no wonder that orderly, law-abiding Afrikaner nationalists turned up their noses at rough radicals who did not abide by prevailing legal norms in their anti-war forays. And within Nationalist ranks there was ever greater consternation at the excessive zeal of the OB in claiming that it had become the vanguard of *volk* aspirations of bringing about an independent republic. For the Malan party leadership, that challenge meant the end of dual membership and other fraternal ties, and after 1941 there was a rift between a party of relative restraint and a movement with a taste for disturbing the streets.

In its most palpable way, opposition to the war meant opposition to soldiers. In the absence of conscription, their voluntary presence sometimes provoked and sometimes mocked OB belligerents, particularly those who from 1940 were banded together in assault squads of Stormjaers, itchy thugs out for confrontation, perhaps defined more by fists than their melodramatic biblical oaths. The setting in almost every sense stirred up caustic passions and tensions. One cause of politicking, within families too, was the decision of about one in three Afrikaners of military age to enlist in the UDF. As with most wars, reasons varied. These included poverty and joblessness among poorer whites who had not been soaked up by interwar 'civilised labour' policies, youthful impulses to grasp war as an opportunity for escape and adventure, and the stir of family soldiering traditions in the reserves. Some unemployed men were instructed by welfare officials to enlist instead of bothering them for aid. The tone of Smuts's mobilisation of fighting morale also had some effect in capturing wavering Afrikaners. Mindful of anti-imperial feeling, the language of address to sway those outside the ranks of the natural 'King's Afrikaners' stressed the ways in which Afrikanerhood was best represented by a proud past of armed heroes and traditions of manly service. Emphasising that standing up for freedom was the Afrikaner way, propaganda messages extolled the *national* meaning of the war effort, appealing to patriotic instincts to defend an endangered South Africa, just as the Springbok rugby captain, Danie Craven, was doing as a volunteer soldier in the UDF.

Apart from recruitment, the public imagery of soldiering commitment also gave cause for provocation. In a perfect symbolic expression of their country's mixed appetite for the conflict, white volunteers did not submit their bodies to armed service unconditionally. Many were choosy, and the government knew well to take account of that politically. Unable to impose a national campaign uniformly, it had to negotiate the extent to which individual servicemen would go to face the enemy. Thus, from March 1940, men joining the UDF (and the SA Police) were requested to take an oath, known as the Africa or 'Red' Oath, obliging them to serve anywhere in Africa for the duration of hostilities. Though it was imposed from May, it remained optional for officers and men already serving, with a large number of those, predominantly Afrikaners, declining to take it, opting instead to stay put as home defence. Those who accepted the oath were identified by deep orange flannel strips on their shoulder pads, the 'Red Tab' iconography of a full soldiering commitment. This was followed by a variant in January 1943, in which a further new oath was introduced for those willing to serve anywhere. Men who had ducked the original 1940 oath were now joined by others who refused to renew it when its terms changed.

For hostile domestic opponents, Red Tab servicemen were too much to stomach. Scrapping for a fight, hotheaded Stormjaers and other civilian toughs got involved in minor brawling in bars and clubs and on the streets with red-tabbed soldiers. When called in to quell fighting between civilians and the soldiers they derided as *Rooi Lussies* or *Luisies*, 'Red Lice', the police could themselves become a needling presence, given their own known factional instincts. They, too, were to be differentiated between those who bore red tabs and those who did not, a tribal code for knowing and trusting who was 'for' Smuts and who was 'against' him.

While most of these running disturbances amounted to small affrays, early in 1941 the OB was in the thick of pitched crowd rioting in Johannesburg. The punch-up spread from fists to bottles, sticks, bricks, bicycle chains and torn-up kerbstones, and the heaving battle was only ended by the arrival of troops and armoured cars. By then, soldiers under attack had also been settling scores, with those on leave from camps around Johannesburg and Pretoria unlikely to turn the other cheek. The offices of prominent anti-war papers like *Die Vaderland* and *Die Transvaler* were attacked, and some soldiers exulted in chasing down and humiliating their opponents, cornering them in alleyways or chasing them up walls and lampposts, forcing them to sing *God Save the King* to avoid being beaten up.

Elsewhere, OB interference with all and any servicemen around tea-rooms, service clubs and other haunts could also court trouble. In Port Elizabeth, RAF navigators and mechanics at an aviation school of the Empire Air Training Scheme walked in pairs, joining fists with men from a nearby RN training school and a hardened assortment of UDF compatriots. As hunting grounds, the larger ports became most dicey of all for circling Stormjaers. With troopship convoys disgorging droves of British, Australian and, later, American soldiers, by 1942 Durban and also Cape Town were housing what Britain's *Daily Mail* of July of that year called 'swarms' of Allied 'locusts'. Any would-be local attackers risked being stripped of more than their dignity. This in turn, of course, also created another little political headache for the Smuts administration, which was doing whatever it could to preserve the peace. It was costly for the government to be seen to be turning a blind eye to some of its Afrikaner citizens – however wilful – being roughed up on their native soil by British and Australian *buitelanders* or foreigners.

In other areas, meanwhile, dissent against involvement in the war persisted. A ban on the private ownership of firearms and the effective confiscation of thousands of rifles at official collection points were hindrances that could be weathered when the immediate objective was not rebellion but a sabotaging of the war effort. There was an incendiary touch of Irish radicalism to some of these actions, involving cutting telephone wires, blowing up pylons and severing electricity lines, bombing post offices, and disabling railway tracks. The most bold, if also harebrained, of these OB strikes was scuppered by the police. This was a 1942 plan to sabotage Durban harbour by sinking a ship at its entrance.

Not for the last time in the history of twentieth-century South Africa would the usual lines that separate criminal conduct from calculated political resistance become blurred. Undoubtedly, for those who were doing the igniting and the demolishing, any criminality was political activity, in that such acts represented protest against South Africa's war and, in particular, opposition to the pro-British basis of its war-making. In this defensive reasoning, aired by a number of radical anti-war Afrikaners, violations of the legal realm of a misguided wartime regime amounted to an implicit expression of political opposition.

Moreover, even as criminality the nature of anti-war violations suggested some observance of limits. Although sections of the pro-war press chronicled these events as rampaging 'waves' of violence and 'deadly' acts of treason, what really distinguished the OB was that it steered clear of anything heinous. Not for it the murderousness of the pro-German IRA of the 1940s, with its tally of killings and assassinations of suspected informants and others singled out for dispatching. When a local bystander was caught in the wrong place and killed in a Transvaal post office bombing, two bungling Stormjaer saboteurs made sacrificial amends for that organisational mishap. Instead of derailing their intended target, a troop train, they accidentally blew themselves up. 'Our objective', declared Kowie Marais, 'was sabotage which would keep troops in South Africa and away from the war.' In another declaration, Marais, who slipped away from the SABC to assemble radio transmitters secretly in Pretoria and Johannesburg, stressed that they 'were told over and over again that we were not to waste lives and, as things happened, less than a handful died'. The OB was hardly angelic. But, in that respect at least, Marais may have had a point.

Although legal proscription was accepted to be far more trouble than it was worth, the authorities remained watchful, regularly probing the movement's sour, violent and shady belly. In this little war based on leads and the capture of subversive agents, implicated fifth columnists included the police, and some 350 members of the SA Police and 60 railways policemen were relieved of duties and arrested early in 1942. The internment of enemy aliens was expanded to net suspects implicated in subversion, and ultimately several thousand were summarily detained.

Among those put away at Koffiefontein, an old Orange Free State mining town, was the head of the OB in Port Elizabeth, B.J. Vorster, who would go on to become a future Prime Minister. What rankled with him was not merely his detention without trial but, as he saw it, that he was being caged not for being 'anti-South African', or 'pro-German', but for the dubious crime of being 'anti-British'. As we know, the brusque detention of political suspects would catch on with Vorster himself in his later apartheid-era ministerial years. The picking off of such militants early in wartime had a dampening effect, but was plainly not the end of emergency nerves. In June 1942, preliminary investigative legal hearings in the Transvaal uncovered the presence of around 8,000 plotting extremists, including members of the police, set on undermining the government.

If extra-parliamentary radicalism was unable to stay the course, it was because it lived too much in its own world, an inspirational world balanced on Berlin and its fortunes of war. As euphoria over what might follow the 1940 defeat of France showed, it was virtually all up to timing and anticipation. The timing was that of German progress. With hopes of German victory evaporating from 1943, the influence of anti-war extremism diminished rapidly. By the end of that year, estimates of OB strength put its dwindling membership at 30,000. Its doughty leader, however, remained an example to faint hearts. Still bullish on the eve of the June 1944 D-Day landings in Normandy, Van Rensburg assured a journalist from *Die Vaderland* of his continuing confidence that Germany would still win the war. By then, the extreme right was already sliding back under the covers with Malan's constitutional nationalism, trimming its more odious anti-Semitic and other Fascist edges to merge into parliamentary decencies.

For many radical Afrikaner nationalists unable to get Germany out of their blood, a vision of its dynamic ascendancy at the expense of an old and shabby Britain seemed to provide some hope that the detested post-1918 world imperial order could be overturned. In a nebulous sense, the Third Reich was to be inhaled spiritually as the new age of progress. For the ultimate realisation of just how flat it had become by 1945, we can turn once more to Kowie Marais, and the almost touching pathos of personal revelation. He had fallen into the trap of backing Hitler, but the Führer had turned out to be 'a disaster'. Most distressing of all, concluded Marais, was that 'the people I had thought to be the heroes of a new era in western civilisation should in fact turn out to be just a band of murderers and nothing else'. His may have been tears of contrition or even circumspection. Or, like Caliban in Shakespeare's *The Tempest*, he may simply have been frothing at the image of his own reflection.

The Canterbury Sails

There is a popular vision of Durban from the decks of arriving British troopships, reflected in on-board newsletters, coded correspondence home (in which South Africa was Yorkshire; and Durban, Doncaster) and cosy reminiscences. It is one of the significant images of what wartime South Africa meant for Allied servicemen – a Natal berth of sunshine, warm civic welcomes, handy brothels, virtually no food rationing, lashings of beer, cartons of cigarettes and, invariably, the Lady in White. Fewer of the stresses and strains of convoy circumstances have been passed on, least of all uglier episodes when Durban ships were rattled by soldiers and airmen who objected to intolerable living conditions. One significant eruption occurred in January 1942, when almost 200 RAF servicemen and soldiers stormed off the troopship *City of Canterbury*, in protest at the atrocious state of their vessel. Built in 1923, the *Canterbury* had been used intensively during 1941, carrying troops in the Middle East and the Mediterranean, and in transporting POWs from North Africa to Durban and South African soldiers to the Middle East. Fitted out to carry 800 men, in December 1941 the ship left Aden for Durban, crammed with over 4,000 Italian prisoners. Such chronic overcrowding and poor maintenance made a complete mess of the *Canterbury*. Some servicemen who had arrived in Durban on an earlier convoy were transferred across for a January 1942 voyage to Singapore. On boarding the *Canterbury* they found themselves wading through layers of coal dust, excrement and vomit. With cabins reserved for officers, lower ranks were funnelled into cargo holds in which Italian prisoners had been cooped up. There they found more of the same, with the bonus of lice, bugs, soiled bedding and defective lifejackets. Local African dockworkers lost no time in voting with their feet. Men sent to work on the *Canterbury* walked off and others refused to take their place. On the quayside, boycotting dockers stripped naked to have lice and fleas hosed off them, while others set fire to infested clothes. Meanwhile, 'mutineering' troops on deck tossed vermin-ridden hammocks and bedding overboard, while a large body of men who had been given shore leave milled about on the quayside, swearing that they would not board the 'hellship' unless it was cleaned up. Panicked, a RAF Wing Commander fired into the air, ordering sentries to fix bayonets to prevent more airmen and soldiers from disembarking. Durban command responded swiftly, strengthening its harbour guard and stationing local troops with Lewis guns on dock walls facing the *Canterbury.* It was a volatile moment, but one which passed in a hush as British diplomats bustled down from Pretoria to meet aggrieved deputations over filthy conditions. Insubordination had to be faced down. But neither could acute needs be ignored. As Durban demonstrated in more ways than one, salt-water morale mattered.

6

What, who, where and why

The Second World War came to South Africa far more than South Africa went out to fight in the Second World War. Indeed, South Africans who went furthest in fighting did not do so in the UDF but by serving overseas in British forces, such as the distinguished RAF air aces 'Sailor' Malan and 'Pat' Pattle, and the decorated bomber pilots John Nettleton and Edwin Swales. And not all, like Malan, proclaimed a national identity by a sewn-in 'South Africa' shoulder lapel or through the display of some tunic springbok badge. There is a natural tendency for historians of this war to exaggerate the fighting actions of their own countries rather than some other bits and pieces that may count as much, if not more, in overall significance. A realistic grasp of proportion is as necessary to an understanding of South Africa's military engagement as it is for that of Romania. There was a fighting disposition but, clearly, not one of sufficient strength to be of anything other

RAF fighter ace of the Battle of Britain: Group Captain A.G. 'Sailor' Malan with African statuette and his pet dog, Peter, reputed to have been a beer addict. (Ditsong National Museum of Military History)

than the slightest significance to the final outcome of the war.

With the benefit of a lull before any opening of a territorial fighting operation, strenuous efforts to make up for the crippling lack of military preparedness paid off, or at least headed in the right direction, even though ground forces were already short of white recruits, despite the beating of every available press, theatre, radio, parade and loudspeaker drum. Becoming increasingly acute, the shortage of white army recruits would plague the government throughout the war, while it refused to sanction the enlistment of black volunteers as regular combat soldiers.

In January 1940, the UDF establishment still consisted of only 1,750 officers and 36,000 men, yet to be fully armed and properly equipped for field operations. Once things got going, the army was able to assemble three infantry divisions as the fighting spine of its land forces. The 7th Motorised Brigade Group of the 3rd SA Division would see amphibious action in the Indian Ocean in 1942, although the balance of the Division would be held back from offensives in order to form a reserve for the UDF's other two Divisions. The 1st SA Division, with armoured cars of the 2nd SA Tank Corps, would participate in the East African campaign, before backing up with the 2nd SA Division to add a string to Allied efforts in the Middle East in 1941.

By the last quarter of 1941, there would be approximately 60,000 Union troops in Egypt, around a quarter of them African and Coloured auxiliaries. This would turn out to be the high point of the Union's ground forces in the war effort as, thereafter, they began to bleed. During the late 1941 Sidi Rezegh battles of the Western Desert campaign, the 1st SA Division would be gutted of one-third of its strength. Early in the following year, the 2nd SA Division would run into obstinate defence in action to take the Italian fortress of Bardia in Libya. Losses sustained came to be dwarfed by the debacle of the fall of Tobruk in June 1942, when 10,772 men were taken prisoner. A denuded 1st SA Division was withdrawn after participating in both of the El Alamein battles, and its survivors would then be reassembled to form the backbone of a new corps, the 6th Armoured Division. In the Mediterranean, it would fight in the Italian campaign from April 1944 through to the end of the war. At the surrender of German forces in Italy a year later, the 6th Division was in Milan, already out of the fight. One of its last moments was to put on a show, parading South African arms on the world-famous Monza Grand Prix motor-racing track. The silence from Ferrari must have been deafening.

The war 'Up North', which these theatres represented, was one in which South African forces did much of the assaulting, on occasion encountering few problems. In East Africa and in Abyssinia, Italian power had clearly been greatly overestimated, for, despite its numerical inferiority, the UDF made a notable contribution to the easy demolition of Mussolini's East African *Imperiale* in the first emphatically successful Allied campaign of the war. In reality, South Africa's well-conducted and fast-moving performance was probably flattered by the rickety position of its enemy, for all Mussolini's expectations of an attack by his army on British colonies in East Africa. Bizarrely, instead of putting its weight into contesting enemy power in Africa, Italy was taken up with the invasion of a sleeping neutral European country, Greece. Its army in Abyssinia may have been enormous, but the majority of its grudging conscripts showed little enthusiasm for a fight. And, unlike what happened in Greece, where flailing Italian forces were rescued by the Germans, Hitler had no interest in sending out an army to try to prevent the loss of Addis Ababa or Italian Somaliland.

Further north, Union infantry participating in a desert counter-offensive against the westerly Italian push into British-occupied Egypt again fared well in opening engagements with Axis forces. Even in the heavily contested move to carry Bardia, the Division sustained only 350 casualties in forcing surrender and scooping up about 7,800 prisoners. Put forward

The King's Afrikaner in classic British colonial headwear: Prime Minister Jan Smuts addressing troops in Egypt. (Ditsong National Museum of Military History)

in the surge to clear the Egyptian frontier positions, it also gave a creditable account of itself, taking 14,000 prisoners for some 500 casualties of its own. Arguably, here, too, the Italians contributed something of their own to their defeat in engagements with Union brigades. All too predictably, Mussolini had spurned a German offer of heavy armour for Italy's Egyptian campaign, as he expected his troops to achieve glory on their own.

The going got very much harder when South African units ran into Field-Marshal Erwin Rommel's formidable Afrika Korps, dispatched to regain the Axis initiative. With Italian Divisions stiffened by an accompanying wave of crack German infantry and powerful tanks, they were mauled at Sidi Rezegh. Chronically short of combatants, the Union could never drum up the reserves to replenish losses adequately. The terminal phase of its desert campaign was equally wounding and humiliating. The small enclave of Tobruk, garrisoned by the 2nd SA Division under the wobbly command of Major-General H.B. Klopper, was surrendered abruptly in June 1942 after a German strike that cut into the town. Perhaps concluding that worse was to follow, Klopper, who had not been spotted by his officers for a fortnight, instructed a bemused Natal captain of the Umvoti Mounted Rifles to run up a white flag. What followed resembled farce. Hesitant but resigned to his orders, Captain Patrick Maxwell stripped off a couple of white bedsheets and clambered into a staff car with an orderly. Zigzagging and ducking down as they came under fire, they made for the lines of the Italian Trento Division. Its commanding general accepted the Tobruk surrender under Klopper's hand from a rueful Maxwell, while shaking his head in bewilderment.

On the face of it, Klopper had meekly handed over tens of thousands of troops to the enemy but had saved his command the cost of a future and futile blood sacrifice. The Tobruk problem was that he had submitted despite still holding some reasonable cards

– over 35,000 troops, thousands of vehicles with ample fuel reserves, plenty of heavy ammunition rounds and sufficient food to have continued to hold out for several months. A little short on perspective, a grumpy Churchill made a meal of the fall. 'One of the heaviest blows' of the entire war, he wrote in his *History of the Second World War*, what it damaged most was reputation: 'defeat is one thing, disgrace is another'. A shock, it was as if a loyal South Africa had handed the Empire a second Singapore. Putting on his best face, Smuts insisted that the country could 'take it', and that with its feet regained it would 'seek retribution'. The cry of 'Avenge Tobruk' now spiced up recruitment appeals but produced no great rush of reinforcements.

All the while, the gruelling slog and harsh privations of the desert war corroded the fighting temper of UDF contingents just as it ate away at British or Australian units. At its lowest point, 1942 was characterised by sliding faith in higher command, low morale, severe rates of desertion, and a mounting individual toll of 'battle fatigue' or chronic neurotic breakdowns. So alarmed was the highly attentive General Dan Pienaar that he even pleaded for the establishment of a permanent court martial in the Union to tackle the rising number of desertion cases being shipped home from the desert campaign.

South Africa's contribution to a frontal fight on

land was virtually spent by the beginning of 1944. Indeed, in January of that year, the UDF did not have a single army formation operating against the enemy. As always, under strength in armed bodies rather than equipment, the General Staff put every particle of planning effort into a further round of active participation. The remnants of infantry regiments, Cape Corps general service battalions and the Engineer Corps, which had served with great success throughout the Western Desert campaign, were cannibalised into forming the Union's last fighting formation.

Participation in the conquest of southern Italy, with its mountainous terrain and large number of natural defensive bunkers for resisting German forces, required whatever infantry could be found to throw into coming battle. This time, the usual search produced a brief stutter. After some deliberation between British and South African command, Smuts agreed grudgingly to the option of organising Coloured servicemen into a Cape Corps infantry brigade to increase the complement of fighting troops for Italy. At the same time, it was also a vengeful little dream come true. He did not have far to look for a commander of the envisaged brigade, pinning the tail on Klopper: he might still be able to vindicate himself after the Tobruk mess by getting a force from Calabria to Rome. But it was not to be, Klopper losing his faint

Italian campaign, 1944: Sherman tanks and support vehicles of the 6th SA Armoured Division trundle across the Arno River in Italy. (Ditsong National Museum of Military History)

chance of personal redemption. The Cabinet rejected the idea of an armed Cape Corps brigade.

As part, firstly, of the British 8th Army and then of the American 5th Army, a still slim 6th Armoured Division took on a spearhead role in the gruelling 1944–5 Italian campaign, racking up a casualty count of over 700 killed and about 2,700 wounded. Effective German delaying tactics made progress slow and costly, not least in their last-ditch holding of the heights at Montecassino, which blocked the Allies' downward sloping road to Rome. There, short of reserves, pressured and under severe strain, the Union

Division kept pressing forward in ferocious storming actions to dislodge the enemy. Depleted further and left exhausted for the last stretch after Montecassino, it not only held together in offensive actions of immense difficulty through a last deadly Mediterranean phase, but performed with distinction across the board, including communications and technical areas.

There is, perhaps, more than a touch of irony that the army of so uncertain a belligerent was part of an Allied campaign relatively modest in size, yet surely significant in that it downed Berlin's chief ally, tethered a German army that was needed for other fields, finished off a Fascist order and put an end to a compromised European monarchy. Slightly less of an irony today is Montecasino, a large, gaudy faux-Tuscan entertainment complex outside Johannesburg where war is that of the gaming machine. Almost unwittingly, it is Cassino without Cassino.

For years before South African forces crossed from North Africa, it was the sea that had carried the war closer to home. There, it faced an obvious dilemma. Italy's entry into hostilities and the closure of the Mediterranean inflated the strategic importance of the Cape route, turning the country's neighbouring oceans into an imposingly large war zone. Without the surface power of a battle fleet, the ocean approaches had to be conceded to the enemy, as puny trawlers and whale-catchers converted for naval use could scarcely venture very far from the sanctuary of home shores.

Within a week of the outbreak of hostilities, trawlers requisitioned by the South African Naval Service (SANS) were carrying out minesweeping operations in Table Bay, while improvised anti-submarine vessels were commencing coastal patrols. In January 1940, following a government decision to create a UDF naval arm, the SANS was absorbed into a newly formed Seaward Defence Force (SDF). This was intended to swallow the South African Royal Navy Volunteer Reserve (RNVR) who were not already crewing British warships. It was, however, not all plain sailing. Many ratings dragged their feet, resenting the loss of the prestige of a RN attachment. Others disliked naval service under a UDF army command. Something of that mood was reflected in the cheeky popular epithet Seaweed Defence Force. Nonetheless, with most teething troubles ironed out, through the 1940s the SDF enlarged its tiny fleet of minesweeping and anti-submarine auxiliary warships to conduct a defensive war as a sort of prolonged maritime siege – the monotonous routine of regular patrolling of the coastline alongside the sudden spurts of explosions, sinkings, rescues and submarine sightings.

The limited reach of the SDF was stretched by the Coastal Air Wing of the SAAF. The effectiveness of the air force's long-range reconnaissance capabilities over the Indian Ocean was enhanced by the arrival early in 1942 of powerful new high-frequency wireless telegraphy sets. The chasing of German submarines and mine-laying auxiliary cruisers in the 1940s imposed a new range of shared tactical responsibilities, including tight coordination between the SDF and the Coastal air force in search and interception as well as in mopping-up actions after passing ships had been torpedoed.

Although there was obviously no enemy fighter challenge to over-sea patrolling, air cover faced any number of other difficulties. While South Africa had access to advanced British and American machinery and its speedy procurement, aircrew had to cope with punishingly long reconnaissance circuits and anti-submarine convoy escort sorties. It was beyond the means of Coastal Air defence command to do much to reduce the cost in fatigue and in fuel, other than to scratch around fruitlessly for watery locations like rivers and *vleis* as better landing spots to cut the Indian Ocean flying times of its Consolidated Catalina flying boats. Existing bases, too, were under increasing strain by the later war years. Runways churned up by over-use made take-offs and landings dicey for Lockheed Venturas and Avro Ansons, while Catalinas could be tripped up by falling lake water levels at St Lucia in

Arthritically slow, noisy and draughty, yet adored by crews: the Avro Anson or 'Faithful Annie'. (www.military-aircraft.org.uk)

Natal. This threatened to impede the capability of coastal squadrons to monitor northwards along the Mozambique Channel, a shipping run endangered by U-boats as well as long-range Japanese submarines. Fortunately, the country's war at sea subsided by the latter half of 1944, before these constraints became severe.

Earlier, by November 1940 the size and conversion quality of the SDF's improvised small warship fleet had become sufficiently advanced for it to supply a minesweeping flotilla of several modern Antarctic whalers for Mediterranean service with the RN. Within the next two years, its continued expansion led to a merger with the South African RNVR establishment to form the South African Naval Force (SANF). By 1944 this had taken on the trappings of a light naval fleet to be reckoned with, at least along Africa's Indian Ocean and South Atlantic waters, able to undertake convoy escort runs between Durban and East African ports. Although SANF strength of 78 vessels by 1945 remained restricted almost entirely to ships with a fishy pedigree, it eventually included three new Loch-class frigates supplied by the Admiralty in the last year of the war. One of these, HMSAS *Natal*, succeeded in sinking a U-boat. Accomplished in English waters on its maiden voyage, this was a big strike overseas for a country not especially famous for a naval tradition.

Naval installations, communications and supply played a key role in sustaining close co-operation between the South African navy and Allied navies. As it was, almost 3,000 South Africans served in the RN, proving their seafaring loyalty even to themselves. Some 2,000 warships tied up at Durban and Cape Town during the war, while a teeming Simonstown dockyard repaired all manner of limping vessels, including visiting heavy cruisers. Some of the technical and administrative chores related to warship services were undertaken by hundreds of white women volunteers of the South African Women's Auxiliary Naval Service (SWANS), established by the SANF in 1943. Feminising, as they did, naval dress and its lower rankings, SWANS recruits mostly substituted for men on ancillary clerical and other maintenance tasks, although some volunteers were selected for technical training. Though it was promoted as a glamorous uniformed service, with posters projecting an almost sensual nautical allure, certain of its postings were hard and demanding. Some women specially trained in range-finding and other aspects of gunnery were deployed to coastal batteries, while others served as harbour defence operators at naval sites like Robben Island.

The contribution of South Africa's little ship navy to its war effort is all too easy to overlook, yet it was probably reasonably equal to its basic task of securing harbours and going after underwater intruders along coastal waters. Although closeness to the RN helped its buoyancy, the Admiralty still never quite grasped the full South African picture. Naturally, it was that of segregation and supply. By the end of 1939, the contortions involved in furnishing separate mess and shore facilities for white and Coloured crewmen so exasperated Rear-Admiral Hallifax in Simonstown that he proposed that all SDF vessels become fully European. That got nowhere. Battling with its shortage of white volunteers, the navy had no choice but to recruit seasoned Coloured sailors from local fishing communities.

A nagging problem of another kind altogether was fish. Whenever enemy mine-laying and submarine

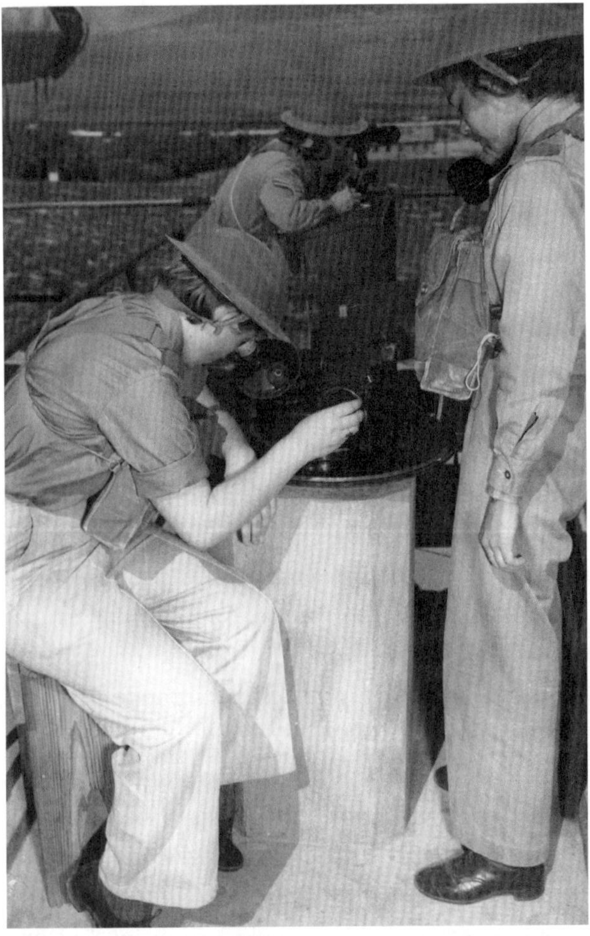

True patriots of False Bay, ready for the Germans: WAAS volunteers in Simon's Town on range-finding watch. (Ditsong National Museum of Military History)

attack threats diminished, tussles broke out between the navy and the fishing industry over the release of trawlers and whalers, as companies like Irvin & Johnson tried to reclaim ships to meet fish demands or to resume whale harvesting for the nitroglycerine essential to explosives production. With a distinctively hybrid warship fleet, this was a navy stuck with the unusual challenge of seasonal demand.

The air force did not have to contend with SAA passenger priorities for its converted Junkers fleet. With equipment deficiencies quickly overcome to the tune of almost 400 aircraft before the end of 1940, and an efficient Joint Air Training Scheme with the RAF to supply about 50 pilots a month for its own cockpits, the SAAF started the war with a flurry of activity to raise output and performance. Once it got going, it never lagged, remaining on a continuous combat footing until 1945. By the end, the air force had about 1,650 aircraft in four wings and 28 squadrons, fed by a hive of air station support units filled by maintenance and construction workers, signals controllers, fitters, armourers, instrument mechanics and refuelling teams.

Behind them, by the early 1940s, was a pool of low-paid white female artisans and aero-mechanics of the Women's Auxiliary Air Force (WAAF), knuckling down to the grime of fitting cylinder heads to the

A springbok of Sidi Rezegh: SAAF Hawker Hurricane fighter pilot of the Western desert Air Force. (Ditsong National Museum of Military History)

Armstrong Siddeley engines of Avro Ansons. Others maintained airfields, doing inspections, installing night flare-paths or taxiing Westland Lysanders. For a time, at least, artisan airwomen with a year's intensive training found themselves carrying out skilled jobs that were customarily the prerogative of male workers with years of apprenticeship behind them. In common with newspaper and magazine portrayals of the service lives of the SWANS and the female lorry drivers and motorcycle riders of the transport section of the South African Women's Auxiliary, 'Winnies' of the WAAF endured depiction of service life as some sort of adventurous finishing school. In it, they walked the fine line of limited liberation from traditional roles, veering between being a decorative skirted presence alongside a Hurricane and a grease-smeared airwoman in overalls.

For their part, the flyers of the SAAF operated under RAF command in East Africa, where they cleared the Regia Aeronautica from the skies, as well as in Madagascar, of which more, presently. Thereafter, the SAAF became a notably robust presence in the desert campaign. Coping with the crudest makeshift base conditions and foul flying weather, its Hurricane fighters and American Martin Maryland bombers contributed virtually a third of the strike capability of the Allies' Western Desert Air Force. As a component of the Allied Balkan Air Force in the central Mediterranean, it went on to inflict significant losses on the enemy, helping to ensure victory in the battle for the Mediterranean. At home, with secure conditions for Allied aircrew training, SAAF facilities in flat areas of the Orange Free State and the southern, northern and eastern Cape played a vital role in maintaining the supply of pilots, navigators and gunners for many theatres of conflict.

Earlier, following Japan's rampant entry into the war in 1941, the Far Eastern game was soon up for Britain. This, in turn, stretched South African nerves. The loss to Tokyo of Singapore and its docking facilities not only increased the strategic importance of Durban. The momentum of the Japanese advance also raised the disturbing prospect of a lunge across the Indian Ocean at Mozambique or Madagascar to try to sever Allied arteries of communication with the Middle East and the Far East around the Cape sea-route. Singapore put Sir Pierre van Ryneveld and his military intelligence on edge, unsure whether the Union would be able to see off an attack by an enemy naval squadron with aircraft carrier support.

As if to confirm Smuts's fretting to Churchill over the inability of the SAAF to screen the Indian Ocean, Vichy French vessels continued to skirt through while, by the middle of 1942, Japanese submarine packs loitering at both ends of the Mozambique Channel were picking off merchant ships with ease. With sinkings only about 500 kilometres north-east of Durban, and the spotting of Japanese submarines and replenishing surface raiders about 700 kilometres from East London, the government became more agitated over enemy forays closing in off the east coast. The consequences of attackers getting in among large convoys lying in the poorly protected waters off Durban were potentially devastating. Nor was that necessarily the end of it. In June, excitable naval intelligence concluded that within a month or so a Japanese stab at shipping in Table Bay was a distinct possibility. There were aerial anxieties, too. In mid-1942 Durban was gripped by panics over the effectiveness of its ground air defences and blackouts after unidentified aircraft were sighted at high altitude, suspected of being snooping Japanese spotter planes.

A local phase of heightened activity sharpened regional strategic thinking. One imperative for British high command was to deny Japan any opportunity to extend its naval and air power in the Indian Ocean. There, the bud to be nipped was the French colonial island of Madagascar, which possessed a large deep-water harbour at Diego Suarez on its northern end, a modern naval base and a Vichy administration in the lap of the Japanese. After reports of Japanese submarines and cruisers berthing at Diego Suarez, the SAAF mounted astonishingly lengthy photo-reconnaissance flights of up to nine hours through raging tropical storms, crossing from the East African coast in lightened Maryland bombers with auxiliary tanks. The results of this high-altitude probing assisted in preparing a precautionary invasion and occupation of Diego Suarez, an action which had been on the cards since the end of 1941.

Putting at Britain's disposal an Army Brigade Group and close air support, Smuts, predictably, wanted to go the whole hog, urging the seizure of other island ports. But his ambitions of using the Allied landing to sneak through the stamp of an oceanic *pax South Africana* were frustrated by Churchill's command, for which the biting off of Diego Suarez was sufficient to block Japan. Assembled in, trained and launched from Durban, the Anglo-South African Operation Ironclad invasion force struck Madagascar in May 1942. This major amphibious invasion by British forces, in which UDF units were pivotal, was the first since the botched attempt to carry the Turkish Dardenelles in the First World War. Although resistance from overwhelmingly inferior French forces was scrappy, retreating defenders had plenty of ground across which to weave, holding out for several months before capitulating. Malaria and mosquitoes aided them in making it difficult for invaders. Not only did the successful capture of Madagascar ease pressure on the long windpipe around the Cape to the Middle East and on the India supply corridor, but it also increased the Union's margin of security from any frontal Japanese threat, though shipping along the Natal and Zululand coasts remained in the sights of Tokyo's submarines.

However improbable the actual prospect, disturbingly loose talk of a Japanese invasion also produced one of the stickier domestic moments of the conflict. As coastal Zululand and even inland rural areas throbbed with rumours of a pending Japanese invasion in 1942, apprehensive intelligence monitors were in little doubt that many disgruntled Africans were virtually readying themselves to welcome the Japanese as a liberating army. Cape Town had its own interesting variation on this theme. In his recent memoir, *A Blow to the Hoop* (2010), the educationist Richard van der Ross recalls a meeting of the Coloured Teachers' League of South Africa at which it was declared that as Japan, a Coloured nation, would be invading the Union, control of the country would pass naturally into the hands of its Coloured people.

Scrambling to try to create a more united country and strike a greater sense of common purpose in the face of foreign menace, Smuts swallowed hard. For the home-front morale of all South Africans to

They also serve who sit and type: Cape Corps orderly on clerical duty. (Ditsong National Museum of Military History)

hold, something had to be done to ease friction over the discriminatory burdens of segregation. Already finding it difficult to police the cities because of the war-induced growth of their African populations, the government suspended influx control (the notorious pass laws which denied most Africans the right of permanent habitation in urban areas) for the duration of the Japanese fright.

It was to be a short-lived, expedient political gesture. For, once the invasion alarm died down, the old segregatory laws were reactivated. This helped to spark a subsequent anti-pass campaign and fanned black political militancy, resulting in the wartime radicalisation of bodies like the Natal and Transvaal Indian congresses, and in the founding in 1943 of the heady ANC Youth League. 'Segregation has fallen on evil days' may well have been the Prime Minister's famously fretful conclusion in his noted speech of that crisis year. It did not mean that its ordinary days had passed. The fighting (and winning) of an impending 1943 'khaki' election in which servicemen's crosses counted, could include the tantalising sop of a more socially inclusive national life, but not the equalising cause of a new nation. In any event, what counted for Smuts in that successful political contest was the – illusory – assumption that the Nationalist threat had been disposed of.

Those earlier invasion worries were also disconcerting for Jan Smuts in another touchy spot. For it found him raising in public the possibility of an official taboo having to be broken. His 1942 position in parliament was that in the event of the country finding itself confronting the emergency of an invasion, all of the UDF's 'Non-European' soldiers might have to be armed. Unsurprisingly, the reaction to this dare was mixed. The response from the prickly edges of anti-war Afrikaner nationalism was fraught. Subject to the impounding of their own rifles in sweeping government action against subversion, compliant farmers had been relinquishing cherished Boer heirlooms. Their bitter reward was the spectacle of a Smuts ready to declare open season for the black majority to cause armed mayhem. That frantic image was captured by a cartoon in *Die Vaderland* in April 1942. Cavorting barefoot warriors were waved on by the Prime Minister to parliamentary assurance that, in the event of any Japanese invasion of the country, he would see to it that 'any Coloured or African person who asked for a weapon would receive a weapon'.

Elsewhere, though, the government's fleeting equivocation over arming was music – however vicarious its sound – to the ears of those who since the start of the war had been demanding that blacks be granted the right of war service on equal terms with whites. For some, with whites perilously split, black inhabitants were the real backbone of survival. What was required was a wide issuing of guns to *all* loyal volunteers. Demanding 'Arms for Non-Europeans' in March 1942, the Non-European United Front imagined the formation of a new armed home-guard citizenry, as '8,000,000 Non-Europeans, Fully Mobilised and Armed', would be a trusty shield to 'Lessen the Danger for All'.

It was also a little capital for the now pro-war Communist Party, its earlier dutiful adherence to the Hitler–Stalin pact and denigration of African soldiering loyalty flushed down the drain of the nearest Left Book Club. With its shoulder to the wheel of an all-out patriotic war effort against Fascism, the party probably had no better time than the war years after 1941. It had Jan Smuts applauding the herculean struggles of the Soviet Union, the SABC carrying the war propaganda voices of its leaders like Bill Andrews, and the authorities relaxing paper rationing for its presses to maintain the pro-war fervour of communist pamphlets, booklets and posters. Publications such as *Inkululeko* promoted not only the romanticised Russian imagery of the Red Army Soldier, but also the heroism of the local, spear-carrying African Soldier, toasted for a steadfast stand against the desecration of his land in pamphlets like *They Served Their Country.* For the Communist Party's exuberant *Give Him a Gun, NOW* campaign *For Defence & Victory* through the issuing of firearms to African soldiers, the government vacillation of 1942 was about as close as it got to any possible fulfilment.

The thorny issue of what a soldier was and who

Cape Corps servicemen sampling the subversion of an Army Education Services reading room: the forward-looking tone of educative British pamphlets like Current Affairs *and* Common Sense *was strongly social democratic and egalitarian. Winston Churchill found such publications politically irritating; Jan Smuts is unlikely to have differed. (Ditsong National Museum of Military History)*

was to be a soldier was the Union's Achilles' heel from the beginning to the end of the conflict. Close to 40 per cent of the UDF enlistment, or that portion which constituted the Cape Corps, the Native Military Corps (NMC) and the further ethnic sliver of the Indian and Malay Corps, were not fully soldiers or not soldiers of the sort who could be called upon to return fire. In the First World War, while African servicemen had been confined to unarmed labour contingents, Cape Corps riflemen had served in combat battalions in East Africa and in the Middle East. And at its rebirth in 1939, its veterans' association pressed that 1914 precedent, laying claim to arms as their due, for were they not even more civilised than the westernised Maori of Auckland?

A quarter of a century later, however, the corrosive political effects of too liberal an organisation for war were deeply inhibiting. Almost without exception, all black recruits served as non-combatant support or auxiliary troops in the Non-European Army Services. While Cape Corps recruitment at least bore a semblance of tact in being entrusted to the Directorate of Recruitment, there was no beating about the bush in arrangements for the NMC. Maintaining fundamental continuities in labour mobilisation, enlistment of Africans was controlled by magistrates of the Native Affairs Department, who found it hard going. The majority of NMC recruits were prised out of poor rural areas, some stricken by drought, with pay (at less than half that of white servicemen) sufficient to draw on some destitute men. That rate grew even more pinched in August 1940, when the Secretary for Defence informed the Chief of the General Staff that the UDF was paying its NMC servicemen too much, and cut the remuneration of an African private to one shilling per day. It matched the cost of a packet of cigarettes.

NMC members rarely struck anything more than matches, being restricted as non-combatants to a myriad of unskilled and semi-skilled support duties, installed as everything from medical orderlies, mess servants, cooks, batmen and painters to transport drivers, mechanics, telephone operators, clerks and guards. Natal took a little advantage of being Natal, with Zulu-speaking white gunnery officers experimenting briefly with the training of some Zulu gunners for a shore battery. It was a rare encouragement of lethal capability. On that score, although also remaining a non-combatant soldiering formation, the Cape Corps was a cut above, providing trained gunners for the Coast Garrison Force, armed security guards, and a pool of skills for motor transport and engineering works companies.

The prominence of the racial factor and of racial inequality in South African forces is, in a way, not much more surprising than that of the US Army with its strict segregation and separate black units raised in the South. What was more peculiar or even fanatical was not necessarily the Union government's insistence on keeping black soldiers disarmed, something which irritated even its more pragmatic General Staff, but its obsession with the *trappings* of weaponry. The Prime

Minister's vintage contribution to the war of the words provoked by that issue came in an early parliamentary exchange over the possible formation of an armed NMC. 'To prevent any possible misunderstanding', Smuts exclaimed, it was 'to be clearly understood that natives will not, under any circumstances, be equipped with arms of precision'. That meant the De Lisle carbine or other modern European firearms. At the same time, it did not mean keeping all auxiliary soldiers completely naked. The drafting of around 30,000 Non European Army Services (NEAS) men into guard battalions, to be stationed at strategic points like airfields, harbours, explosives and chemical plants and to secure Italian prisoner-of-war camps, required that they guard with something. The inspired solution to the arming of non-combatants was, as Smuts put it in the House of Assembly in June 1940, to equip them in a manner 'fitting of the traditions and customs of the natives'.

What that implied was illustrated in photographs and propaganda documentary film which showed masked guardsmen training for gas warfare while bearing spears or guarding Bristol Beaufighters with clubs. Behind the badge of a tribal nationhood, it would be up to African battalions to keep invaders or fifth columnists out, and Italian captives in, with wooden clubs, fighting sticks and light spears. For an enraged ANC president, Alfred Xuma, it was contemptible, a 'mockery' for Africans to be 'expected to fight aeroplanes, tanks and army artillery with knobkieries and assegaais'. To a no less effusive if more disingenuous Secretary for Native Affairs and his rural magistrates, it was the entirely admirable opposite. Far from being demeaned or emasculated by not being placed under modern arms, Military Corps soldiers were being given the opportunity to resurrect the honour of a lost warrior tradition.

Weapons to spear chests and crack skulls were the ancient tools of proud Zulu and Xhosa warriors, the pre-colonial heritage of the region's foot soldiers. In a sense, it was a way of war that was being restored, as African guardsmen were decolonised and returned to an elemental, pre-colonial world of familiar militarism, shorn of alien mechanical technology. As various rhapsodic messages declared, the 'aboriginal' weapon swung by the 'aboriginal' arm could be counted on to do an effective job. Of course, this did not wear very convincingly. The problem was that the harder the authorities tried to talk up this bizarre element of their defensive effort, the more ridiculous they appeared to some of those they were most trying to persuade, including soldiers themselves, who felt demeaned.

South Africa was never able to find, let alone favourably exploit, the true balance of its main fighting

Soldiers apart: Trainee African recruits of the NEAS armed to ward off the threat of the Axis industrial war effort. (Ditsong National Museum of Military History)

forces. Some developments, like the political inability to impose conscription and the lukewarm response to voluntary recruiting, would or could have been foreseen. But the fixed operational problem was always the idea of a war waged by a bolstered combat elite. To ensure that white combatants were freed for the front line and kept fully effective, they would be subsidised by a second string of unarmed black servicemen to shoulder more flat-footed tasks, such as cleaning the latrines or digging tunnels.

From the perspective of British and other Allied forces with their low ratio of about one to ten between combat troops and service or pioneer corps soldiers, the formation of the UDF is especially striking. Peculiarly, it gave South Africa's pose in the Second World War something of the social flavour of early modern European warfare, in which Christian soldiers were free voting citizens while others were servile nonentities. Here, the Union's white and black hierarchies were obviously riddled by layers of prejudice, indifference and patronising 'European' applause of unexpectedly strong soldiering performances by 'Natives' and 'Coloureds'. Yet they also contained their own minor measure of simple decencies and civilities. It was there in the 1943 plea from the NEAS Directorate for NMC auxiliaries to be acknowledged as soldiers and not regarded as labourers. It was there, too, however paternalistically, in the moral liberalism of individual army officers who recognised the personal history, honour and dignity of the attending Corps men to whom they were bound. It is that ordinariness and awareness of a common humanity which resonate in the writer Guy Butler's bleak poetic tribute in 1945 to a 'Cape Coloured Batman', portrayed as 'the man the Empires made', fated to be 'left without hope in History's shade'.

DAN PIENAAR

Major-General Daniel Hermanus ('Dan') Pienaar was one of the Union's most prominent military commanders until his death in an air crash in Kenya in 1942 on his way back to South Africa. Born in Natal in 1893 and trained as an artilleryman, Dan Pienaar joined the UDF in 1913 and served in its expeditionary forces in German East Africa and in Palestine. After 1918 he combined military leadership and administrative responsibilities, holding a range of command and staff posts. A strong-minded figure and an accomplished tactician, in the Second World War his first front-line assignment was command of the 1st South African Infantry Brigade in the 1940–1 East Africa campaign. Pienaar was then given battle in the 1941–2 North Africa campaign, where his leadership played a role in the engagements of Sidi Rezegh and Gazala, desert operations of considerable military significance. In March 1942 he took command of the 1st SA Infantry Division, directing it in the testing actions of the battle of Gazala, the retreat to Egypt, the defence of El Alamein and the last decisive battle of El Alamein. His effective generalship was recognised by the award twice of the Distinguished Service Order and by his military appointment in November 1942 as a Companion of the Order of the Bath for his role in the 'magnificent achievements of British and Dominion Troops and their Commanders' in the Middle East. Pienaar earned a merited reputation as an inspirational, no-nonsense commander, popular with his troops, both white and black. His relaxed manner, sometimes moody yet always fair-minded temperament, known fondness for drink and fluent English and good Zulu in addition to his native Afrikaans, contributed to his renown as an adored general, keeping him in the news not only in the local press but also in overseas papers like the *Daily Telegraph* and the *Chicago Tribune.* Still, the Pienaar image is not all one of heart-warming heroism. Desert warfare was not exactly a bed of roses for the Division and its commander, and its appalling conditions took a high toll. Pienaar was also the target of a whispering campaign within British command. It suggested that following South African losses at Sidi Rezegh and in the Tobruk debacle, Pienaar lacked the nerve to thrust his infantry into a tough and risky offensive.

Yet nothing dimmed his national popularity and near-legendary status, expressed in his symbolic role as a powerful, charismatic Anglo-Afrikaner warrior commander, implicitly the Springbok figure of those patriotic wartime packs of Springbok cigarettes. It was not only desert campaigning that helped to construct that image. Domestically, too, Dan Pienaar was an influential part of the picture. Fiercely anti-Nationalist, he threw himself into recruitment drives, squaring up to anti-war opposition and spreading his curt message that Italy and Germany were a threat to the Union which could only be dealt with by expelling them from Africa completely. Mercurial and individualistic, Pienaar nursed parliamentary political ambitions. Had an East African accident not claimed his life, who knows?

7

Gain, pain and wane

If it is true that South Africa started off in the war on the wrong foot, it is equally true that not only did it stay on its feet, but it prospered from the conflict. One obvious factor was that, unlike most countries, it escaped economic upheaval. Another was that, like many countries, it reaped the benefits of a speedy war-induced industrialisation which fattened government tax earnings and increased provision for spending. Possibly more important than either of these elements, however, was the possession of gold. It was that which easily enabled the Union to finance its war effort. Already producing one-third of the world's gold at the outbreak of war, South Africa was able to sustain and even to increase its output of bullion through the war years. Coupled with a steady increase in the wartime gold price, production enabled Pretoria to generally cover the costs of its war involvement. And there was also more to those favourable circumstances.

The foreign exchange brought in by booming exports and healthy annual surpluses of state revenue over expenditure throughout the war provided a financial windfall with which to reduce national debt. Unlike Britain's war experience, South Africa's was not one of battling to say afloat by borrowing heavily and running up enormous deficits. It was more a celebration of the luck of being able to pile up gold reserves, and of the war as a valuable means of settling the burdens of debt, both government and private.

Jan Hofmeyr, Smuts's Minister of Finance, bided his time before crowing over this. With Britain convalescent and facing the humiliating prospect of a devaluation of sterling, it would have been bad form. But good news had to be broadcast, and Hofmeyr did this in an early postwar budget speech which noted that South Africa's 'territory has been spared the ravages of war', and that its 'financial and banking structure has stood the strain'. Even more beneficially, 'our foreign exchange reserves are soundly invested in a sufficient gold reserve', and 'as a state we have ceased to be a foreign borrower'. As to the future, the Union's 'ability to buy from the world the goods which we do not produce at home is not limited, as is the case with so many war-torn countries, by a lack of internationally acceptable money'. All in all, then, as mainly a trader South Africa did extremely well from the war.

Domestically, there were also other kinds of fruitful movements. The number of people in military uniform always played second fiddle to the enormous expansion of the civilian workforce, especially after 1940. It was there, far more than in some bread shortages or in the slow pace of housing provision which annoyed the white electorate, or in other domestic alarms, that the war had its major impact. Crucially, it greatly intensified the pace of both black and white urban immigration and the expansion of manufacturing industry, trends which had been growing since the economy began to recover from the 1930s depression. With up to 200,000 whites from a labour force of 790,000 away on various military duties, the need for increased industrial output to meet wartime demand could only be sustained by the employment of more African workers, and their numbers rose by three-quarters during these brisk years. As the tide of workers, increasingly trailing their families, swept into many towns in an unplanned and chaotic way, the urban black population increased by some half a million to almost 1.7 million by the end of the war.

Pressure-cooker economic mobilisation suddenly opened up an unimagined range of previously closed work opportunities to semi-skilled black factory workers, such as machine operators, and to white female 'emergency' workers, who were used extensively in munitions plants, although at lower pay for the same job. Comparatively speaking, before demobilisation and the return of white ex-soldiers to manufacturing, black workers in semi-skilled and factory operative jobs fared well as they knocked on an open door. Where it mattered, the government could not allow the industrial war effort to be hampered by severe labour shortages. Simultaneously, the chance momentum of war inevitably brought aggravation elsewhere. Most newly urbanised black workers with an appetite for factory wages had deserted mining and farming, raising a constant chorus of complaints of labour shortages from those sectors. In the Western Cape, for instance, there was squealing from wine and fruit farmers that canning factories and Cape Corps recruiting were poaching their vineyard and orchard labour.

Overall, this sea-change was both bewilderingly sudden and complex in its consequences. Although miners' wages were depressed during the war, labour shortages pushed up the earnings of black factory workers significantly from the early 1940s. Moreover, the impact of some wartime policies led to a narrowing of the wage gap between white workers and black workers. The usual bargaining strength of white labour was eroded by War Measure 9 of 1942, which prohibited strikes by white workers until the end of the war, and by the priority given by the state to the need of stable industrial growth for the war effort. At times, this even meant increases in minimum wages to head off a downing of tools by black workers. 'The maintenance of industrial peace', stressed Ivan Walker, the Secretary for Labour, 'is essential when the country is at war.'

Indeed, wartime brought broad recognition that productivity and efficiency could only be assured by more decent basic living standards. By 1940, the Department of Labour's Wage Board was mostly leaving white workers to find their own feet, while tending to the need to raise wretchedly low unskilled wages through minimum wage legislation and the introduction from 1942 of minor cost-of-living allowances. At the same time, militant black trade unionism with a strong foothold in manufacturing industries added muscle to the push for improved wages, increasingly to counter the squeeze of rising inflation. With a combined membership of almost 160,000 workers, the many industrial unions represented by the Council for Non-European Trade Unions pursued numerous disputes, shrugging off the 1942 War Measure 145, which sought to curb the strike rights of black workers. Still, although at a peak by 1944, trade unionism was hard pressed to hang on to its gains after the end of the war, and was soon floored by the harsh suppression of the 1946 African mineworkers' strike.

Equally, deep underlying social problems were worsened as wartime circumstances aggravated rather than eased deprivation and inequality. With virtually no provision of basic services for the migrants swarming into towns, shack settlements sprawled and wretched slums expanded into ever larger pockets of stunted urban life. As the flurry of industrial war production unsettled the customary segregationist landscape of white towns and African reserves, the Smuts administration confronted a seething urban crisis of health, housing and educational need. Its response to it all was faltering and ambivalent. While committed to the system of racial segregation, the government displayed some faith – or much delusion – that the improvement of social conditions for the unfranchised majority could be achieved without the indigestible cost of any serious extension of political rights.

If it was not the reforming wartime faith in a universally beneficent welfare order symbolised by Britain's famous 1942 Beveridge Report, the Smuts administration's tinkering with social reform and reconstruction nonetheless envisaged recognition of a more common public need. Its forward-looking Social and Economic Planning Council of 1942 dripped reforms, including school feeding provision in 1943 and the universal provision of pensions, though still at racially discriminatory rates. In another shift, general state funding was used to finance urban African education, and by the end of the war Hofmeyr, Smuts's deputy, was advocating free mass schooling for African pupils. Elsewhere, there were efforts to arrest deteriorating health conditions; the Minister of Health even favoured the introduction of a national health service with free, universal access. Earlier, wide reforms backed by the 1942 Smit Committee on the Social, Health and Economic Conditions of Urban Areas intimated that there was a fair amount to play for, including complete abolition of the pass system, lifting low wage levels, and financing improved housing and health provision for urban black inhabitants.

Of course, these 1940s aspirations for a new and more socially inclusive shape to South African society flared briefly and then fell, soon to be swept aside decisively by apartheid. Few might have met the 'Africans' Claims in South Africa' of the increasingly impatient wartime ANC. Spurred on by that banal and toothless Anglo-American declaration of high-flown principles, the 1941 Atlantic Charter, which it adapted 'from the Standpoint of Africans' and adopted as policy in 1943, the Congress wanted 'full citizenship rights such as are enjoyed by all Europeans in South Africa'.

Such absolutes were never there to be met. Even so, it is difficult to miss the way in which liberal-minded and even moderately radical white English and Afrikaner South Africans shared in the general progressive mood generated by the strains and searchings of the war. In subscribing to the notion of a fairer future, they joined the many worldwide who, in living through the painful war years, became receptive to ideas of planning and greater social fairness in the making of a safe and secure future after the defeat of Fascism.

The most emblematic setting for this was, of course, a Labour Britain in 1945. With part of Britain's middle-class officer corps radicalised and turned social democratic by the educative experience of a can-win war against totalitarianism, captains and majors, some still in uniform, turned out as prospective left-wing parliamentary candidates after VE Day. Of course, South Africa's war could not have been expected to produce electoral platoons of socialist firebrands. What it did was to encourage many of its more decent white servicemen to take stock. Wartime education nudged them in that direction, to reflect on ideas of change for the better. In 1941, the General Staff established an Educational Corps steered by reform-minded figures such as the Director of Military Intelligence, Lieutenant-Colonel E.G. Malherbe (later Principal of Natal University), and the Active Citizen Force officer and liberal philosopher, R.F.A. Hoernlé, an interwar founding member of the South African Institute of Race Relations. The Army Education Service, like those of other Allied armies, and the local servicemen's newspaper, *Fighting Talk*, impressed upon audiences that the war that they were in was not only against Fascism, but was for democratic principles and the road towards a more common society. At the very least, it sought to cultivate an enlightened spirit as the basis for building an optimistic new postwar order, one which could be held together by a wider sharing of the cake of citizenship. In the end, change would come soon with the end of Jan Smuts's ancien regime, but not in the better way that those soldiers had fleetingly envisaged.

As for others, black as well as white, most were weary of war and fixed on the ordinary pleasures of peace. As in so many other warring societies, in 1945 the pull of any New Jerusalem politics was felt far less than the more prosaic realities of the end of service life. In the transition from war to peace, distant European and North African demobilisation was far from easy. Previous jobs were not necessarily still open, and advice or support was not always available. Neither were those who returned all treated as heroes, including those who adopted that pose. One who worked feverishly to pass himself off as a war hero was Potlake Kitchener

Leballo, the future founding secretary of the Pan Africanist Congress, who manufactured a dashing war record of survival at sea, imprisonment in Germany and infantry service in the British army. Probably the epitome of the more bruising legacies of the good war against totalitarianism was the discriminatory dividend for patriotic service. To black soldiers went the predictable scraps. These included, for those Native Military Corps members who had secured a job on demobilisation, the delivery of bicycles to help them on their way. That act quickly took on the insulting aura of Smuts's bicycles. There was always something cringingly colonial – or more than faintly Victorian – about it. As a war service gratuity, it was not a question of what it offered – transport to save men from a bus queue. It was what it stood for.

Just Nuisance

It is just conceivable that Just Nuisance was the most idealised dog of the Second World War. An enormous Great Dane, enormous even by Great Dane standards, he was certainly a strange case of four-legged fashion. Born in the southern suburbs of Cape Town a year before Nazi Germany swallowed Austria, this starred canine was acquired by a Benjamin Chaney, later accompanying his owner when he moved to Simonstown to run the United Services Institute. Its patrons, mostly naval ratings, immediately took to Just Nuisance, and he to them. Ties were lubricated by regular walks and incessant snacks. In addition to sponging off Royal Navy employees, the dog took to following sailors back to the naval base and its dockyards. There, he took up the life of Riley, lounging about on the decks of warships and often snoozing across the top of gangplanks. Disdaining to move for anyone trying to embark or disembark, Just Nuisance soon became known simply as Nuisance. A comforting, hand-licking weapon in South Africa's maritime arsenal, the sneaky Nuisance enjoyed complete liberty of movement, and regularly accompanied sailors on train journeys to Cape Town. Although repeatedly turned out of carriages when he was discovered by irate conductors, an undeterred Nuisance would simply take his chance with the next train carrying seamen. Or he would lope along to the next station where he would curry favour and board an indulgent carriage. Reeling RN sailors were enough of a headache for the railways without having to cope with a dog that had got above its station. Chaney was warned to control Nuisance or else see him put down as a public pest. With war around the corner, this was poor timing for the spirit. The solution was distinctively British – phlegmatic and slyly mocking. News of the official threat to Just Nuisance prompted sailors and local civilians to petition the Navy, imploring it to do something to secure the dog's future. One offer was to buy Nuisance a railway season ticket. However, Simonstown command decided to enlist him officially as an 'Able Seaman' in August 1939, making the Great Dane the only dog ever to be officially in the Royal Navy. With mock seriousness, his trade was listed as 'Bonecrusher' and his religion as 'Scrounger'. From 1939 to the dog's death and burial with full naval honours in

1944, AB Seaman Nuisance was attached to the shore establishment, HMS *Afrikander.* Entitled to free rail travel through Navy service, Nuisance continued to accompany sailors on boozy train journeys and provided a nose to help in getting them back from bars through the coastal blackout. A popular boost to naval morale, Nuisance was a canine balm which fitted into a healthy world of doting men and devoted dogs, abnormal seaside normality away from utterly abnormal oceans. Today, like a rock on a rock, a statue in Simonstown commemorates his canny life and its link with a once ubiquitous British Navy. A more surprising variant is the current English rock band, Just Nuisance, which uses his image and cautions dogs against loud barking during its live concerts.

Courtesy of Gareth Smit

8

Postscript

By your feet shall you remember them

On 23 June 2011, an elderly Englishman named Nathan Clark died in New York. A shoe designer and manufacturer, he was a member of the famous Clark family, Somerset Quakers who since the 1820s have been a British family firm synonymous with good-quality, comfortable footwear. After serving in a Republican ambulance unit during the Spanish Civil War, Clark joined the British army's Service Corps in which he served through the North Africa campaign. By then already an enthusiastic foot engineer, he had been struck by the utility of Spanish peasant espadrilles and by enclosed Indian Pashtun sandals, more durable and more flexible over sand and rock than standard-issue army boots.

In the Western Desert after 1941 Nathan Clark's eye was also taken by something else. South African desert war veterans were especially addicted to locally sourced, rough suede ankle boots with easy lacing and thick crepe-rubber soles. Pliable and well cushioned for wading through deep sand, they were being run up by Egyptian cobblers in Cairo to replace worn-out South African boots. In effect, they were an adaptation of the *velskoen.* Intrigued, a scheming Clark traced boot patterns in the belief that the improvised desert footwear of some of the men of the 1st SA Division could be turned into leisurewear in peacetime.

At the 1947 Chicago shoe fair, Clark's desert boot swept the board as authentic reproductions of British and Commonwealth footwear, African suede the colour of stewed tea and squelchy East Asian plantation rubber. Exported to Western Europe in the 1950s and 1960s and then worldwide, Clarks desert boots have sold over 15 million pairs, mostly in their definitive sand colour, have been worn by Bob Dylan and have been regularly rediscovered by the fashion industry as ordinary non-fashion. Its wartime origin probably not widely known, the desert boot is, in a way, the unsentimental and universally unnoticed heritage of South Africa's campaign contribution Up North. Unlike Klopper's Tobruk, Nathan Clark's enduring product is a walking memory of servicemen who once found a deft way of staying on their feet.

Select secondary sources and some further reading

J. Ambrose Brown, *The War of a Hundred Days: Springboks in Somalia and Abyssinia, 1940–41* (Ashanti, 1990)

P. Bagshawe, *Warriors of the Sky: Springbok Air Heroes in Combat* (Ashanti, 1990)

G. Butler, *Bursting World: An Autobiography, 1936–45* (David Philip, 1983)

M. Cardo, '"Fighting a Worse Imperialism": White South African Loyalism and the Army Education Corps (AES) during the Second World War', *South African Historical Journal*, 46, 1 (2002)

J. Crwys-Williams, *A Country at War, 1939–1945: The Mood of a Nation* (Ashanti, 1992)

S. Dubow & A. Jeeves (eds.), *South Africa's 1940s: Worlds of Possibilities* (Double Storey, 2005)

J. Fennell, *Combat and Morale in the North African Campaign: The 8th Army and the Path to El Alamein* (Cambridge University Press, 2011)

P.J. Furlong, *Between Crown and Swastika: The Impact of the Radical Right on the Afrikaner Nationalist Movement in the Fascist Era* (Wesleyan University Press, 1991)

P. Furlong, 'Allies at War? Britain and the 'South Africa' Front in the Second World War', *South African Historical Journal*, 54, 1 (2005)

N.G. Garson, 'Smuts, the South African National War Museum and 1947', *Military History Journal*, 10, 6 (1997)

I. Gleeson, *The Unknown Force: Black, Indian and Coloured Soldiers through Two World Wars* (Ashanti, 1994)

A. Grundlingh, 'The "King's Afrikaners"? Enlistment and Ethnic Identity in the Union of South Africa's Defence Force during the Second World War, 1939–45', *Journal of African History*, 40, 3 (1999)

L. Grundlingh, 'The Recruitment of South African Blacks for Participation in the Second World War', in D. Killingray & R. Rathbone (eds.), *Africa and the Second World War* (Longman, 1986)

W.K. Hancock, *Smuts: The Fields of Force, 1919–1950*, vol. 2 (Cambridge University Press, 1968)

W.K. Hancock & J. van der Poel (eds.), *Selections from the Smuts Papers*, vols. 6–7 (Cambridge University Press, 1968)

C.J. Harris, *War at Sea: South African Maritime Operations during World War II* (Ashanti, 1991)

R. Hyam & P. Henshaw, *The Lion and the Springbok: Britain and South Africa since the Boer War* (Cambridge University Press, 2003)

A. Jackson, *The British Empire and the Second World War* (Hambledon Continuum, 2006)

J. Keene (ed.), *South Africa in World War II: A Pictorial History* (Human & Rousseau, 1995)

D. Killingray, *Fighting for Britain: African Soldiers in the Second World War* (James Currey, 2010)

J. Lambert, '"Their Finest Hour"? English-speaking South Africans and World War II', *South African Historical Journal*, 60, I (2008)

R. Lyman, *The Longest Siege: Tobruk* (Macmillan, 2009)

J.S. Mohlamme, 'Soldiers without Reward: Africans in South Africa's Wars', *Military History Journal*, 10, 1 (1995)

A. Paton, *Towards the Mountain: An Autobiography* (David Philip, 1980)

I. Phimister, 'South Africa, Union of', in I.C.B. Dear & M.R.D. Foot (eds.), *The Oxford Companion to the Second World War* (Oxford University Press, 1995)

N. Roos, *Ordinary Springboks: White Servicemen and Social Justice in South Africa, 1939–1961* (Ashgate, 2005)

N. Roos, 'Education, Sex and Leisure: Ideology, Discipline and the Construction of Race among South African Servicemen during the Second World War', *Journal of Social History*, 44, 3 (2011)

E. Rosenthal, *Japan's Bid for Africa: The Madagascar Campaign* (Libertas, 1944)

G.R. Rubin, *Durban, 1942: A British Troopship Revolt?* (Hambledon Continuum, 1992)

C. Somerville, *Our War: How the British Commonwealth Fought the Second World War* (Weidenfeld & Nicolson, 2001)

South Africa at War Series, 1939–45, 8 vols. (Purnell, 1968–1979)

I. van der Waag, "The Union Defence Force between the Two World Wars, 1919–1940', *Scientia Militaria*, 30, 2 (2000)

I. van der Waag, 'Smuts's Generals: Towards a First Portrait of the South African High Command, 1912–1948', *War in History*, 18, 1 (2011)

Index

Abyssinia 17, 69, 71, 106
Active Citizen Force (ACF) 43
African National Congress (ANC) 63, 134, 146; Youth League 127
Afrika Korps 107
Afrikaans Burgher Commando 43
Afrikaner Rebellion 88
Agar-Hamilton, J. 23
Andrews, Bill 129
apartheid 23, 25, 26
Atlantic Charter 146
Attlee, Clement 61
Auxiliary Defence Corps 19
Battle of Britain 65
Berlin Olympic Games 38
Beyers, Major 54
Bogart, Humphrey 26
Botha, General Louis 47
British Broadcasting Corporation (BBC) 85
British Union of Fascists 40
Bunting, Brain 38
Butler, Guy 136
Campbell, Roy 17
Canaris, Admiral Wilhelm 85, 86
Cape Corps 110, 126, 130 -2, 136, 143
Chamberlain, Neville 59, 70
Chaney, Benjamin 150
Childers, Erskine 86, 87
Churchill, Winston 21, 109, 122, 124
Civic Guard 80
Civilian Protective Services 80
Clark, Nathan 153, 154
Collingham, Lizzie 14
Communist Party of South Africa (CPSA) 16, 17, 63, 129
Craven, Danie 92
Cromwell, Oliver 67
Crosby, Bing 26
Dadoo, Yusuf 63, 64
Davies, Norman 18
Dear, I.C.B. 21
Defence Rifle Association 43
De Waal, Brigadier Pieter 35
Dubow, Saul 23
Duncan, Sir Patrick 56, 57
Dutch Reformed Church 89
Dylan, Bob 154
Eden, Anthony 70
El Alamein 105, 138
Emergency Measures 50
Emergency Regulations 51

Fields, Gracie 26
First World War 34, 39, 41, 45, 48, 81, 124, 130
Fisk, Robert 27
Foot, M.R.D. 21
Fourie, Jopie 88
Gaddafi, Colonel Muammar 27
Galpin, George 59
Goering, Hermann 38
Great Depression 31
Great Trek 64
Grundlingh, Albert 24
Hancock, Sir Keith 9, 11, 19
Hankey, Sir Maurice 35
Hertzog, General J.B.M. 25, 29, 55, 57, 69, 81, 82, 83
Hitler, Adolf 10, 37-9, 56, 59, 62-4, 88, 106
Hoernlé, R.F.A. 148
Hofmeyr, Jan 141, 146
Holm, Erik 85
Imperial Airways 37
James, Sid 25
Jarvis, Captain H.G. 54
Jeeves, Alan 23
Just Nuisance 25, 150-2
Kathrada, Ahmed 63
Kemp, General J.C.G. 55
Kempf, Walter 86
Kitchener, Lord 44
Klopper, Major-General H.B. 25, 27, 108, 110
Krige, Uys 17
Lady in White 77-9
Lass, Colonel J.C. 83, 84
League of Nations 11
Leballo, Potlake Kitchener 148
Leibbrandt, Sidney Robey 25, 38, 84-7
liberation struggle 23
Liebenberg, B.J. 24
Lloyd George, David 39
Low, David 37
Lynn, Vera 25, 79
Madagascar 121, 122-5
Malan, Group Captain A.G. 'Sailor' 103
Malan, Dr D.F. 25, 57, 81, 82, 90, 91
Malherbe, Lieutenant-Colonel E.G. 147
Mandela, Nelson 36
Marais, Kowie 83, 96, 99
Martel, Gordon 21
Mawdsley, Evan 21
Maxwell, Captain Patrick 108
Military Nursing Service 19
Montecassino 35, 111, 112
Mosley, Sir Oswald 40
Mtirara, Chief Mhlohlo Mvuso Matanzima 62
Muggeridge, Malcolm 73
Mussolini, Benito 37, 106, 107
National Liberation League (NLL) 16
National Museum of Military History 8, 101
National Party 23
Native Military Corps (NMC) 9, 130
Native Representatives 61
Non-European Army Services (NEAS) 133, 135, 136
Non-European United Front (NEUF) 63, 128
Overy, Richard 18
Ossewabrandwag (OB) 83-90, 93-8
Pan Africanist Congress (PAC) 149
Paton, Alan 58, 59, 89
Phimister, Ian 21
Piel, Else 32

Pienaar, Major-General Daniel Hermanus (Dan) 25, 109, 137-9
Pirow, Oswald 25, 31-41, 49, 55, 81
Progressive Party 83
Purified National Party 81
Reitz, Deneys 55
Robben Island 117
Rommel, Field-Marshal Erwin 107
Royal Air Force (RAF) 100-3, 119, 121
Royal Flying Corps (RFC) 41, 45
Royal Navy (RN) 28, 49, 94, 117, 150, 151
Royal Navy Volunteer Reserve (RNVR) 48, 113
Russell, Seán 86
Salazar, Antonie 37
Schoeman, B.J. 65
Seaward Defence Force (SDF) 113, 115, 117
Shakespeare, William 99
Sidi Rezegh 120
Siedle, Perla *see* Lady in White
Smuts, Field-Marshal Jan 8-10, 18, 25, 30, 35, 41, 45, 56, 57, 65-7, 69, 70, 87, 93, 107, 122, 124, 127, 129, 133, 141, 145
South African Air Force (SAAF) 45-7, 71, 76, 113, 119-21, 124
South African Airways (SAA) 37, 47, 119
South African Broadcasting Corporation (SABC) 83, 96, 129
South African Institute of Race Relations 148
South African Naval Force (SANF) 115, 116
South African Naval Service (SANS) 48, 113
South African Police 50, 76, 92
South African Red Cross Society 36
South African Women's Auxiliary Service (SWANS) 116, 121
Spanish Civil War 16, 17, 22
Spies, S.B. 24
Status of Union Act 29
Statute of Westminster 29
Steer, George 17
Teachers' League of South Africa 125
Tobruk 26, 105, 108, 109, 111, 138
Tolkien, J.R.R. 25
Union Defence Force (UDF) 23, 28, 30, 33, 41, 43, 48-50, 57, 74, 75, 79, 83, 91, 92, 94, 102, 104, 106, 109, 110, 113, 128, 130, 131, 136, 137
United Party 55, 56
Van der Poel, Captain 26
Van der Ross, Richard 125
Van der Spuy, Major-General Kenneth 45
Van Rensburg, Johannes (Hans) 85-7, 90, 98
Van Ryneveld, Major-General Sir Pierre 41, 42, 74, 122
Vorster, B.J. 97
Walker, Ivan 144
Waterson, Sydney 31
Waugh, Evelyn 87, 89
Weinberg, Gerhard 21
Women's Auxiliary Air Force (WAAF) 118, 119, 121
Women's National Service Legion 36
Xuma, Alfred 134